Hiking Trails in the Pacific Northwest

by Amos Wood

Greatlakes Living Press, Publishers, Matteson, Illinois

Hiking Trails in the Pacific Northwest

Printed in the U.S.A.
International Standard Book Number: 0-915498-36-7
Library of Congress Catalog Card Number: 77-71554

Greatlakes Living Press, Publishers, Matteson, Illinois

Contents

Acknowledgements

No book is the sole work of the author. Inspiration and assistance come from many sources. In this case, inspiration came first from outdoor recreational activities of hiking families, like our own, who took to the hills to become a part of the Pacific Northwest heritage. It was prophetic that Elaine and I had our first date hiking Mount Rainier's Emmons Glacier trail. Inspiration also came from the organized activities of The Mountaineers and from its stable of talented authors like Louise B. Marshall, Harvey Manning, E. M. Sterling and accompanying photographers, like Bob and Ira Spring and Keith Gunnar. Other hikers' writings have been equally helpful.

Our youngsters Dick, Francie and Nancy, all active backpackers, have each added their bit. Partner Elaine, playing devil's advocate, kept the manuscript drafts honest, and Frances Hodge offered valuable assistance. Able editorial guidance was provided by Robert E. Oestreich, whose love affair with the Cascades is longstanding. Sam Foster did miracles in his photo laboratory in Oregon.

Finally, for all those kindred souls that we met on the trail and conversed with on this subject of mutual interest, our special thanks and gratitude.

Introduction

Where is the eastern boundary of the Northwest in the United States? I've tried to find a source that would give the answer without success. Old literature indicates that in fur-trading days a region known as the Northwest was located in an area bordering the eastern Great Lakes. The Northwest image gradually moved west as civilization moved west—to the western Great Lakes region of Wisconsin and Minnesota and finally to the Oregon Territory.

The Pacific Northwest is not a well-defined geographic region even though certain portions of it seem to be well established in the minds of their local residents. It is generally accepted, however, that the Pacific Northwest includes at least the western portion of Washington, Oregon and British Columbia.

My concept of the Pacific Northwest is that the southern and northern boundaries ought to be expanded to include northern California's Klamath Mountains and southeastern Alaska, respectively. The eastern boundary would extend beyond the Klamath and Cascade Mountains, and the rugged coastline of the Pacific Ocean would form the western boundary. In other words, the region would extend from Mount Shasta in the south to Skagway, Alaska in the north and include much of what is in between. My definition includes a region approximately 1400 miles long and 200 miles wide.

The hiking opportunities in this region are unlimited. Thanks to a moderate climate, there are a great many hiking devotees, young and old, who try new trails all year.

Hiking seems to be synonymous with this geographic region. The natives accept hiking activity as a regular part of their lives without giving it a second thought. Those who have migrated here get caught up in the infectious enthusiasm of the hiking fraternity. Visitors from other parts of the country, who sample some of the hiking opportunities here, soon regard the region as a hiker's paradise.

The hikes described in this book barely scratch the surface of all that are possible. How were they selected? Of 8000 possible trails, why these few? No reasonably-sized volume could contain all that is known about the hiking trails in this region. My foremost purpose is to present, from this wide array, only those hikes that, in addition to being representative, have historical or geographical significance. I chose a wide variety of hikes that vary in elevation from sea level to tree line. They include the seashore, the mountains and the flatlands in between. There is excellent hiking literature already available regarding this beautiful alpine region.

A related purpose is to include a variety of hiking experiences that can be enjoyed by anyone between the ages of three and 73. Some can be completed in a few hours in ordinary clothing and comfortable walking shoes, and others require the most sophisticated gear.

On first examination, such a mixture of hikes may well infuriate the dedicated Sierra Club card carrying member, disturb the avid beach walker and puzzle the incurable backpacker. However, I am sure that all outdoor people, on further contemplation, will appreciate our inclusion of material concerning the geological wonders of the area as well as our enthusiasm for the great sport.

1

Pacific Northwest Hiking

The Pacific Northwest provides opportunities for extensive outdoor recreational activities. It has been said that most residents in this region tend to be both water and mountain oriented in their outdoor pursuits. Many who enjoy photography, camping, fishing, hunting, beachcombing and mountain climbing find that hiking can be a pleasant part of these activities. Some even consider backpacking as a means to pursue related interests. Others backpack solely for the sheer enjoyment of setting up camp, living outside and making do with what is carried in their pack. The average breadwinner eagerly looks forward to the holidays when he or she can commune with nature. However, much hiking can be done without backpacking—it all depends on the length of the hike. If we go on an overnight, then we backpack.

Hikes can be endurance tests but should not be attempted by the beginner. Hiking can be done with nothing more than comfortable shoes and clothing attuned to the probable weather for that day. If your hiking is to be done on unknown trails, which may contain rock or beach gravel, a good pair of hiking boots is essential. If the hike is to be undertaken in a dry area, a canteen or water bottle is a must.

If you know where you are going, what your objective is and likely weather conditions, special precautions are not necessary. If the terrain is such that you might get lost, emergency items are important such as a map and compass, emergency food, matches and fire starter and tarp for possible overnight shelter. I knew a forester who curled up under a tree and slept without taking off his hat, John Muir style, but this is unlikely for most of us used to civilization's comforts. Since only a few of us know how to eat off the land, food supplies are required for an overnight—and that includes water.

Because of an increased number of hiking enthusiasts in the Pacific Northwest and due in part to extensive literature on hiking, facilities in those trails that have been publicized and popularized are being saturated. Most of these facilities are in the region's national parks. Already there is concern for the environment in many national park and wilderness areas. The current procedure of reservation requirements at

A well-outfitted group of backpackers hikes along a Pacific Northwest trail.

Stan Bettis photo

some of these popular campsites is considered by some to be evidence of facility shortage. Overnight camping, with its normal demand for campsites, campfires and toilet facilities and other comforts, may well become a thing of the past at these overworked sites. One day hiking, beginning and ending from our automobile trunk compartments, may become popular by necessity. In any event, we can expect more restrictions in the future, and this is good reason to avoid national parks.

My family has been hiking and backpacking in the Pacific Northwest region for more than thirty years. The beaches, foothills and alpine areas are old haunts. We have learned to love the Cascades, Olympics, the solitude of Vancouver Island, the serenity of the Queen Charlottes and the grandeur of Alaska. We hope to expose much of this to our children. Except for the few crowded campsites, Mount Rainier National Park being one, there exists a thousand other secluded sites to explore.

Most of us hike or backpack at our leisure. Only a few favored rangers, guides and timber cruisers make a living from hiking. Thus we reserve time for hiking on weekends and during vacation periods. Many people will plan a different hike for each weekend from a priority list. Others may sneak in only a few hikes during the year. Hikes will cover wide types of trail-hard packed ocean sand beaches, needle-packed forests, crushed rock in mountain terrain, cobbles of all sizes in glacial moraine, rock slabs measured in tons, paved roads with gravel shoulders and even cedar planked walkways over marshes. So in our spare time we experience contrasting footpaths as different as the type of country we choose to hike in.

Hikers and backpackers have natural enemies. These are not bears or cougars but instead are the trail bikes, four wheel drive recreational vehicles and snowmobiles. Local restrictions and regulations govern their use. Trail bikes are prohibited in national parks and national forests. On the highway many motorcyclists appear to be backpackers. Few motor bikes, however, are seen parked at trailheads. Instead we see sport cars and vans.

PACIFIC NORTHWEST CLIMATE

A major factor contributing to the widespread interest in hiking throughout this region is the gentle climate. It may be presumptuous to generalize about the climate of an area extending from northern California to southern Alaska, but the climate of this enormous territory is surprisingly consistent.

Climate extremes common to areas of the same latitude are not found here. At sea level and west of the Cascade Range the winters are less severe, and the summers are not as hot as elsewhere.

For example, a check of national weather data for a typical January day shows only a 10 degree spread (36-46 degrees) throughout the Pacific Northwest covering recordings from Eureka, California, to Juneau, Alaska, and going inland from the Pacific coast at Astoria, Oregon, to Spokane, Washington. For this same day much of the northeastern part of the country had 40 degrees below zero weather, and the ground around the Great Lakes region was frozen 16 inches deep!

There are three principal reasons for the Pacific Northwest's even climate. The first is the immediate proximity of the Pacific Ocean. Circling the North Pacific Ocean Rim, the massive and relatively warm Kuroshio Pacific Ocean current runs parallel to North America's west coast at about the latitude of Vancouver Island. Here the major portion of the current turns south along the shores of Washington, Oregon and California and creates relatively warm and stable temperature patterns. A secondary portion of the Kuroshio Current near Vancouver Island turns north and gives southeastern Alaska its relatively even climate.

The second reason for the region's even climate is geographical. All along this portion of the west coast are mountain ranges that parallel the coast approximately 100 miles inland. The Coast Range of northern California, the Cascade Range of Oregon and Washington and the Coast Mountains of British Columbia all act as major buffers to air mass movement and thereby tend to establish a steady coastal climate. The Olympics also affect climate.

A third reason is the effect of high altitude—high-velocity jet streams traveling across the North Pacific Ocean Rim. These high-speed air masses indirectly control Pacific Northwest climate through coastal rainstorm activity. The eastbound paths of these jet streams fluctuate and change paths. When they do, they produce marked effects on other parts of the United States. Unseasonably cold weather in the central and eastern States may accompany droughts in southern California and Colorado.

Thus the influence of Pacific Ocean currents with their even temperatures, the protective geography of coastal mountains and the effects of stratosphere jet streams all make for a steady climate and favorable all-year hiking conditions. However, within 200 miles of our island home, there are variations in climate from the 200-inch annual rainfall in the wet coastal rain forests, to Paradise Valley on the southern flanks of Mt. Rainier, which is the snowiest spot on earth (a record of 80 ft.) to dry sagebrush country in the Columbia basin with annual rainfall amounts as low as six inches.

Such are the choices for the ardent hiker. Mountain area hikers prefer the summer months because of ready access to alpine levels with breathtaking vistas, wild flowers and attendant wildlife. Conversely, ocean beach hikers select the winter months because of the abundance of beach driftwood and opportunities for beachcombing flotsam from the Orient. Thus the climate of the Pacific Northwest is conducive to hiking pleasure any time during the year.

PACIFIC NORTHWEST WEATHER

Generalizations about climate are based on known prevailing differ-

The Wenatchee Mountains viewed from Mission Ridge near Wenatchee, Washington.

Pat O'Hara photo

Tunnel through rock outcropping was originally cut by a real estate developer. Now, it offers an interesting route for beach hikers.

ALW photo

ences in the region's weather. There can be sunshine on the seacoast of Vancouver Island, a grey drizzle overcast in Seattle and arctic conditions at the 4000 foot elevation at Timberline on Oregon's Mount Hood.

In this portion of the United States many outdoor recreational activities, like hiking, are pursued constantly. Boating, golfing, fishing, hunting, climbing and beachcombing are pursued every season. Within much of the Pacific Northwest region lawn grass and shrubs stay green throughout the year. In the years to come, the mildness and evenness of the weather may cause roses to bloom in January. Some deciduous trees lose their leaves as late as December and are followed by budding and other signs of spring in January. Thunderstorms and high winds are rare in this region. The exceptions occur principally in the mountains. Seasons in the Pacific Northwest tend to blend together. The overcast weather is a refreshing change for everyone. (Admittedly, this region is no place for the sun-worshipping hiker.) With proper clothing, hiking can be enjoyable in the Northwest mist. Interestingly enough, Seattle's annual rainfall is less than that for most eastern cities, but it is stretched out more evenly with a greater number of overcast days. Fortunately, the hiker is faced not only with a mild climate but also with mild weather.

Most mountain ranges of the Pacific Northwest create their own local weather. The coastal mountains of Washington, Oregon and British Columbia all produce a lush growth of trees and brush on the west, or windward, side. The northern California redwoods are partly a result of coastal fog and drizzle. Alaska Sitka Spruce generally grow in a narrow band all along the Pacific Coast under special environmental conditions. Dry, clearer weather is the norm on the east, or lee, side of the mountains. On both sides south, the facing ridges are warmer and generally make for better campsites.

Local areas have unique weather patterns. In the lee of the Olympic Mountain Range is the so-called "banana belt" where the annual rainfall is only 15 inches per year, one tenth of the coastal rain forest rainfall on the windward side. At sea level the Pacific Ocean coastal weather has its well-known rhythmic sequences. Lowland lakes often present characteristic daily wind patterns. Foothill regions have their own weather moods. Mountain regions generate weather personalities of their own.

A friend of mine once said that most residents in this region are either mountain or water-oriented recreationalists. This means that one may have an alpine interest while another will follow saltwater or freshwater marine activities. Further, these interests rarely seem to be combined. One needs only to watch mountain highway traffic and lowland boating traffic on weekends to confirm this opinion. Life in this region is exciting, and hiking the region's trails is part of the adventure.

Elaine and I need no greater incentive on a Saturday morning to

Cobble beach in Oregon leading to Bay Ocean Area. Hikers should be sure-footed.

ALW photo

leave our sea level Mercer Island home on Lake Washington, with its nearby trails, than the lure of glacier rimmed Mount Rainier 55 miles to the south or the snowcapped Cascade Mountain Range 50 miles to the east or the huge ice cream peak of Mount Baker 100 miles to the north or the white saw-toothed Olympic Range 60 miles to the west. We cancel our plans, and there is just enough time to grab our boots, put a lunch together and head out. On other days our planned hikes may start out in fog or rain. What an elated feeling to start from dreary weather and emerge into brilliant sunshine after a hike.

WEATHER REPORTS

In this region the average hiker is not necessarily discouraged but guided by weather reports. He is pragmatic and says, "So it may rain today; that will not spoil our planned trip to . . .."

Government weather reports tend to be conservative. Weather forecasts that are reported hourly give wind direction and velocity, temperature range and percent chance of measurable precipitation. Here, daily weather reports include atmospheric temperature data as background information for hunters, skiers, climbers and fishermen. Occasional temperature inversions also are reported.

A helpful aid in determining weather conditions near a hiking location within a 100-mile radius is to set your FM radio dial at 162.55. This band is reserved for detailed weather observations and other information given in sequence for the region's weather reporting stations. A 24-hour service is available in most reasonably populated areas. It may cover the exact area where you plan to hike.

WEATHER SIGNS

When you follow weather patterns, both adverse and favorable trends can be predicted. Atmospheric changes generally react systematically and follow established patterns. The weather is not as unpredictable as you might believe. Its Indian signs, or known associations with wind direction and cloud formations, foretell the day's probable weather. Many of the region's "weather saws" are quite reliable. Some of these are:

Mount Rainier cap means rain after nap.
With a northeast blow watch for snow.
North wind shift, away the clouds will drift.
When cirrus sail across the sky, in 48 hours it won't be dry.
Northwest winds are short and sweet, for they bring flotsam to your feet.
When lenticulars fill the sky, east winds come from country dry.
Clouds of mammatocumulus shape mean rain soon without debate.
Perihelion, night or day, means rain not far away.
Mackerel sky, not long dry.
Dew on morning grass chases away rain fast.
Rain before seven, clear before eleven.

In a town located in central Oregon a local weather forecasting system, which has a credible record for accuracy is used. Each morning the local radio newscaster peers out his window and notes where a herd of goats is grazing. He has observed that the degree of good weather is related to the height that the goats climb. The higher they go, the better the weather. The newscaster claims the goats do an excellent job of forecasting the weather.

In general, this region is blessed with the onshore flow of moist marine air from across the Pacific Ocean being undisturbed by terrain for thousands of miles. Watching cloud development, changes in wind direction and barometric fluctuations enable us to forecast the weather. Hikers in this region can go comfortably almost anywhere at anytime if they will protect themselves against possible rain and wind and take into consideration the chill factor. This applies at sea level and at foothill and alpine levels.

We hike every week of the year. Even during the Christmas holiday period we, and many others, will be hiking the lower elevations. Be weather conscious and plan for weather fluctuations.

2

Regional Hiking Tips

Back in the 1930s The Mountaineers organization initiated an annual climbing course. A list of Ten Essentials was drawn up for climbers' use and, in effect, has become law for Pacific Northwest outdoor activities. This list applies to all backpackers, less so for overnighters on a well defined trail and only slightly for a person who takes an afternoon walk in a bird refuge. They should be reviewed, however, for every hike.

These Ten Essentials are listed in order of importance. A check for all these items should be made when you get out your hiking boots and assemble other gear.

- *Extra clothing* - Even though it is sunny when you start out, take that extra wool sweater and plastic sheet for windbreak use or emergency shelter.
- *Extra food* - Lightweight emergency food for several meals is easily added to the regular meals you plan.
- *Sunglasses* - They are needed for many trail conditions on rock, sand and snow.
- *Knife* - For most hikes a Boy Scout-type is sufficient.
- *Firestarter* - When a fire is needed, weather conditions are usually at their worst. Figure on building your fire in wet, windy weather with wet wood at night. Thus, you will need fuel tablets and candle pieces.
- *Matches* - Put a dozen or more in a waterproof container. Kitchen matches and a small strip of rough sandpaper are better than a match pad.
- *First-aid kit* - Assemble or buy one from the recommendations of mountaineering groups. It should include bandaids, gauze pads, adhesive tape, salt tablets, aspirin, needle and a first-aid manual.
- *Flashlight* - Best is the two-cell with spare batteries and bulb.
- *Map* - It should be one portraying the immediate hiking area that gives detailed information on contours and landmarks. Expendable xerox copies of specific portions of larger maps and charts are helpful for each member of a hiking group.

A variety of packaged dried foods for two-week alpine backpack hiking trip for three people through the Olympic National Park is shown spread out. Packages are divided up for stowage into individual packs. First in, last out is the rule to avoid constant repacking.

Author photo

- *Compass* - An inexpensive compass is ideal, but you remember that magnetic variation increases throughout the Pacific Northwest with corresponding changes in latitude.

In addition to the Ten Essentials, there should be a list of Ten Desirables, but no Committee of The Mountaineers ever tackled that one. I don't think that any two people would agree on what ought to be included. Avid backpacking author and friend Archie Satterfield once compiled such a check list containing 61 additional lightweight and desirable items. He felt most of us would have these items after a season of hiking. Our list for the Ten Desirables, not in order of importance, are:

moleskin - for blisters
whistle - a shrill, police-type for emergency use
insect repellent - for mosquitoes, flies, etc., in lowland and alpine elevations
sunburn lotion - zinc ointment and chapstick
repair kit - needles and thread, safety pins and pliers

nylon cord - 50 feet is always needed
nylon rope - for rigging food caches
folding saw - for tent poles, cooking fires and beachcombing
towel - for general use and *pencil and paper* - to keep a brief diary and leave notes.

In the Pacific Northwest a place exists that can be hiked any time of the year. Some months are better for particular areas. For example, a winter storm on the beach may bring in an array of treasures while a winter storm in the mountains may make the area impassible. This is our general timetable for the year.
January - Washington foothills and beaches; *February* - Oregon foothills and beaches; *March* - British Columbia beaches (Vancouver Island and Q.C.I.); *April* - Washington Puget Sound Islands and bird refuges; *May* - Washington foothills below snow line; *June* - Northern California Cascades; *July* - Oregon Cascades; *August* - Alaska and British Columbia wilderness areas, upper Cascade lakes; *September* - Cascade and Olympic alpine areas; *October* - Lower Cascades and foothills for fall color; *November* - Coastal lowlands and headlands and *December* - Urban trails and foothill lakes.

Backpacking requires careful planning and packing. For a longer trip with a group, a pack inspection check the previous night with the aid of bathroom scales is a necessity. If there are youngsters in the group and this is their first time out, a good gauge is that a ten-year-old should be able to carry his own clothing, sleeping bag and utensils. A 15-year-old should be able to manage 20 pounds while a sturdy woman should be able to carry 25-30 pounds. The average man should be able to manage 35 pounds. However, it is not how heavy your pack is but, instead, how light that is the cause for admiration.

Age	Pack Weight Range
5	0-5 lbs.
10	19-15 lbs.
15	15-20 lbs.
20	35-50 lbs.

You should hike with people of the same temperament and hiking ability. The pace of the hike is all important. Some like to charge as fast as human endurance will allow, while others prefer to savor every turn of the trail. Some do not want to sit down, while others thoroughly enjoy to stop frequently to do some reading. It is difficult to have these people hiking together.

During a hike to the Olympics with three people, the leader wanted to cover a lot of mileage. His goal was to be able to do 15 miles the first day. He found nothing to do in camp. His two companions were homesteaders and were more interested in arranging the campsite to

Author Amos L. Wood ready for overnight hike. Wool sweater, ideal for winter use, was knitted by Indian woman of Cowichan Tribe on Vancouver Island, B.C.

Duane Oyler photos

test out their new equipment. They enjoyed an afternoon nap and a little reading.

Among people eating habits also differ. One may eat everything he can get his hands on, another only at meals and another may nibble constantly. There are those who can prepare and eat breakfast and break camp in short order, while others are not so adept. Setting up camp and cooking the evening meal are equally simple for some. Usually those new to hiking will bring too much food, sometimes the wrong kinds, but most hikers learn they do not have to eat so much. Elaine and I do not eat a lot, but we do eat often while hiking.

If you are ever caught out in a thunderstorm, avoid tops of ridges and individual trees. Take cover at lower elevations in areas of even tree growth if possible. When there is a choice, head for the firs—not under or near a cedar tree. Cedar trees are more likely to be hit by lightning than fir trees since the firs' pointed needles dissipate the earth's static electrical charge considerably faster than the blunt needles of the cedar. Many a tall cedar has been damaged by lightning.

To be successful, a hike should be planned in advance. Never decide in the early afternoon to take an overnight in the Cascade or Olympic mountains. There just isn't enough time to do everything. First, in the hurried gathering of equipment, essentials may be forgotten. Second, the food is usually makeshift, shy of some items and with unbalanced substitutes. Third, the cameras may not have film, and what you buy en route may not be what is best for that day.

By the time you get to the trailhead, the best part of the day is gone. Several miles in, the first campsite is already full, and it is getting dark. There is no substitute for taking adequate time to collect gear, plan menus and get ready. The before-dawn departure and early morning hike into an area always is rewarding.

Leave the schedule loose so that you can explore the side trails on the way in—better yet from a base camp. If you wait to do your exploring on your way back to the trailhead, you may run out of time and steam. Schedule your return to the trailhead at sundown in order to make the most of your time in the hills. This coupled with some time to stretch out and rest before starting the drive home leaves only a short time before darkness sets in.

Informative Oregon State Park cedar marker post gives direction and mileage along trail.

Author photo

BEARS

Bears inhabit portions of the Pacific Northwest. They are especially fond of wild berries, honey and salmon. Their population increases as one travels north, indicating that northern California has the fewest and southeastern Alaska the most. We have listened to numerous first-hand reports by hikers and have studied accounts of those few encounters that resulted in fatalities. We have concluded that bears can be quite dangerous.

While hiking national parks or forests, you should check with the regional park ranger to determine the tentative population and habits of bears, since park rangers are quite knowledgeable on this subject. Bears are protected in national parks, but control measures are employed when they become nuisances. When hiking other areas, contact state game officials for background information.

The wary hiker will not walk needlessly into a confrontation with a bear. If you happen onto a bear cub, do a rapid turnabout so as not to come between sow and cub. General experience indicates that when a bear smells a person, he will avoid rather than attack. It is well known that bears are continually on the prowl for food. Consequently the overnight hiker should always cache his pack and food well away from the tent and well off the ground.

If a bear invades your camp, there is the old-wives tale concerning banging pots and pans to chase it away. Most backpacking is done with a minimum of utensils, so they are not apt to be readily available. Once in camp you should respect the bear's right-of-way. While searching for food a bear will raise havoc with your gear. A friend experienced this when he returned to camp from a side trip and found most of his gear destroyed.

One writer recommended attaching several small bells on the outside of the pack to announce one's arrival to all creatures of the forest. Other friends, new to overnight camping, did this. During their first hike they met up with a park ranger who greeted them with a laugh and remarked, "I see you read that book." The following morning the bells were stowed well inside their packs. It seems neither of our friends had particularly cared for the incessant bell jingling. Incidentally, they have yet to see a bear in five years of hiking Washington State.

We have had several encounters. One night while camping in British Columbia our tent was knocked down by a bear who left his muddy claw tears on the nylon covering and bent one of the aluminum corner posts. Our food was cached well away from the tent. Another time we encountered sow and cub on a Pacific Ocean beach in Washington. There was a steady onshore wind, and we knew the bears could not catch our scent, so we did a quick turnabout. On another occasion in British Columbia we saw a bear 50 yards away from our campsite, but it ambled on without noticing us.

An acquaintance with two small daughters had taken a Sunday afternoon hike in the Mount Baker National Forest in Washington. In the curve of a trail they suddenly met a good-sized bear. The father stopped in his tracks and quietly motioned that his daughters do likewise. The bear also stopped and stood up, full height, licking his mouth and nose with his long, red tongue. The father's heart pounded furiously. Almost immediately the bear got down on all fours and ran away. The bear merely had moistened his nose to confirm the human scent, which admittedly must have been stronger than usual.

In southeastern Alaska the brown bear follow the salmon migration up stream. They are adept fishermen and manage quite well even in shoulder deep water. Obviously when hiking these regions it is best to avoid such streams. Above all, follow the precautions suggested by local residents.

Despite the occasional encounter, bears should not limit your hiking plans. Many hikers have yet to see bear signs let alone the perpetrator. With the hundreds of thousands of hikers annually hiking our alpine regions, foothill forests and ocean beaches, their experiences, or lack of them, prove that we can live in harmony with these animals.

GOLDEN AGE PASSPORTS

The National Park Service is now issuing free Golden Age Passports for senior citizens, 62 years or older. The card permits free lifetime entrance to those national parks, monuments and recreational areas that charge entrance fees and are managed by the federal government. The passport card also provides a 50 percent discount on federal use fees charged for facilities and services such as camping, boat launching, parking, etc. The passport does not cover fees charged by private concessioners.

This Golden Age Passport, now being issued by the National Park Service to senior citizens, will permit lifetime free entrance to those national parks, monuments, and recreational areas which charge entrance fees.

Author photo

The card admits the permit holder and a carload of accompanying people. Where entry is not by private car, the passport admits permit holder and his or her spouse and children.

To obtain a Golden Age Passport you need to apply in person. They are not available by mail. At the time you apply, you must show proof of age. A state driver's license is acceptable as long as it shows your birthdate. A birth certificate is acceptable.

The passport is available at most federal recreation areas, where it may be used. Therefore it is not necessary to obtain one before taking a hiking trip in one of the national parks. These passports may be obtained in person at National Park Service headquarters in Washington, D.C., regional offices and areas of the National Park System where entrance fees are charged. These passports also may be obtained at Forest Service regional offices and at most Ranger Station offices of the Forest Service. Even the Bureau of Land Management District Offices and recreational areas have them. They are not available at post offices.

There is a similar pass called the Golden Eagle Passport that is available for people under 62 years of age. With this passport there is a $10 annual charge that allows the permit holder to bring in a carload of accompanying people. This passport is available at the same offices as the Golden Age Passport and has essentially the same restrictions for its use in national parks, monuments and recreational areas that charge entrance fees. This may be an advantage when the hiker is visiting a number of national parks or may be visiting the same park numerous times.

In the Pacific Northwest the following National Park Service areas have entrance fees:

California:

John Muir National Historic Site; Lassen Volcanic National Park; Muir Woods National Monument; Pinnacles National Monument; Sequoia-Kings Canyon National Parks and Yosemite National Park.

Oregon:

Crater Lake National Park.

Washington:

Mount Rainier National Park.

HIKING PHOTOGRAPHY

Most hikers and backpackers in the Pacific Northwest rate picture taking as one of their main joys of trail hiking. Good pictures of scenic attractions help in the sharing and reliving of a particular afternoon beach walk, a day hike to the foothills or a weekend backpack trip in alpine meadows. Most hikers become hiking photographers, and many photographers take to hiking trails for subject material. Hiking in this region is synonymous with picture taking, and no coverage of outdoor hiking would be complete without some mention of it.

Why bring a camera? The answer is abundantly clear on your first hike when you come across a fawn ahead on the trail, approach a field of avalanche lilies, note a windswept tree at sunset silhouetted against a shimmering ocean or take in a breathtaking view of a snowcapped mountain. During every hike there are images to capture—the natural beauty of the far scenery, the close-up detail of a flower, activities of your fellow hikers and the day's surprises. There is the wide variety of subjects from sea level to ski level with challenges to overcome while recording them.

Regarding equipment, our technology has made possible readily available, lightweight, compact and reliable cameras of excellent performance that are easily carried in your outer jacket pocket. Pity the Edward and Ashel Curtisses of the early 1900s and their logistic problems with trail travel while carrying the ponderous view cameras of their era.

For the hiker and backpacker, lightness and compactness in equipment comes first. Many who have lived with the weight and clumsiness of earlier equipment now can own cameras like the Minox 35 and Rollei 35. These are fixed-lens cameras of very compact dimensions and are lightweight. They are high quality instruments and are completely self-contained with built-in light metering. The Minox weighs only about seven ounces and the Rollei is somewhat heavier at 13 ounces. This can be contrasted with typical single lens reflex 35 cameras that weigh from 35 to 40 or more ounces. There are excellent cameras from less prestigious manufacturers, which cost less. The prospective purchaser might want to explore a few of these models.

Leightweight camera ideal for hikers weighs less than 7 ounces and is easily carried in an upper pocket.

Leitz Leica photo

For the more sophisticated hiking photographer who demands interchangeable lenses, the Olympus OM-1 is a very small lightweight camera of the single-lens reflex design that features lenses of many focal lengths as well as compact and light in keeping with the camera design.

A good lens for most hiking subjects is the 50mm, while the 135mm telephoto and 24mm wide angle lenses are good accessories. The 135mm lens makes for a reasonable telephoto for wildlife and distant scenes. The 24mm lens is excellent for sweeping views when in the mountains.

Accessibility and operational time in taking a picture is very important to the hiker. He needs the camera to be immediately available at all times. The newer and smaller units fit easily in an outer jacket size pocket or shirt breast pocket, and thus will not interfere with normal hiking or backpacking gait. For those who wish to have their cameras hung around the neck, an effective camera device that keeps the camera from banging against one's chest (and possibly helping throw a hiker off balance) is the Kuban hitch shown in the accompanying photograph. Note that with this strap arrangement, the camera can be pulled up instantly to eye level without having to remove the straps.

I am a member of the hiking fraternity that uses two cameras—one for black and white and the other for color. This provides coverage for slide presentations and show prints. I use identical cameras and rarely have missed the coverage I wanted due to any mechnical malfunction. After a seven mile hike, you certainly want to be assured of adequate coverage. Before I learned this, I once accidentally dropped my only camera on a rocky trail while hiking the Klamath Mountains. I have not been able to retake those pictures that I lost.

I believe taking an absolute minimum of equipment on hikes. Although it is easy to be excessive particularly on the shorter hikes, it always pays to thin down your photography equipment to the bare essentials—except film. Always take twice the amount that you normally use.

Regarding filters, a single skylight filter is needed to cut down high altitude or seascape bluishness. An orange filter is adequate for black and white work.

BINOCULARS

I used to brush aside the idea of carrying binoculars because of the weight, but that has changed. During the past few years, progress in optics has produced different approaches to binocular design. There are now lightweight units of modest physical dimensions capable of giving good performance. From the popular 7x35 (meaning magnification power and diameter of objective lens in millimeters) and 6x30 units, miniaturization has produced ultra-light weight 6x18, 6x20 and 8x20 designs that retain quite good brightness characteristics, which

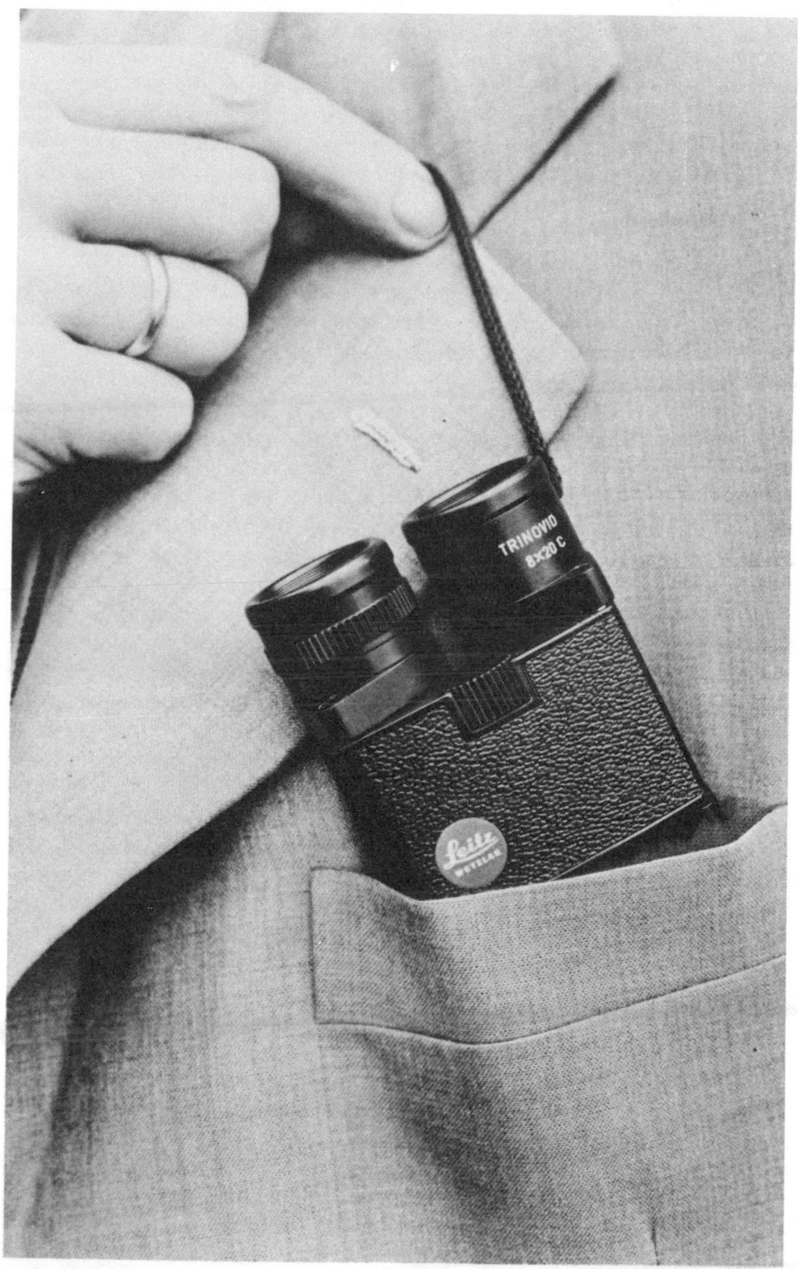

Leightweight binoculars ideal for hikers weigh only 6½ ounces and fit easily into upper pocket.

Leitz Leica photo

are important in marginal light conditions.

The new 8x20 Leitz-manufactured pocket binocular is the champion in the miniaturization contest, weighing a scant 6½ ounces. It has no prisms—the bane of the older and bulkier·models. There also are other lower cost glasses that give good performance such as the Nikon line.

It is wise that the hiker consider these pocket minis. They easily can be carried in your outer jacket pocket in an ever-ready carrying case for quick use, as opposed to the former never-ready location somewhere in your backpack.

Why carry binoculars when hiking the Pacific Northwest? To begin with, there is simply so much to see from great distances. Experience dictates many good reasons: to pick out distant detail, to watch game and birdlife, to study terrain, to watch mountain climbers where vistas allow and to check landmarks. The true test of superior optics is gleaning pleasure while looking at a majestic mountain, like Mount Rainier, for hours, absorbing the detail and not feeling any eyestrain. Regarding the resolution of fine detail, the inexpensive ones do not have this capability. A side-by-side comparison viewing of two different sets is convincing. In the clearer air at higher elevations, binocular use at night for studying the moon and planets is another hiker's pleasure.

A good example of binocular use was told by a friend, who had been hiking about 20 miles east of White Pass in the Snoqualmie National Forest. He came up over a ridge and suddenly noticed what seemed to be a mirage—a strange group of shimmering objects to the east. Chimneys with smoke seemed present in the haze. An immediate check with binoculars identified the apparition as being Yakima, Washington, some 30 miles away.

It is satisfying to have good optics that can be carried comfortably while hiking. The best of the new miniature binoculars have all the fine qualities. Their precision alignment minimizes eye fatigue during an extensive vista study or a continued sweep of a particularly exciting landscape. This alone proves the worth of such an investment.

3 Beach Hiking Pacific Ocean Shores

Because much of the Pacific Northwest borders the Pacific Ocean and since several beach hikes are covered, some general information on hiking ocean beaches is useful.

Backpacking on dry, sandy beaches is harder and slower than trail packing. The damp region between the water's edge and the dry sand is the easiest part to walk on a flat, sandy beach. Gravel beaches (where agates are) promote difficult footing. If the beach contains cobble size rocks, watch for sea growth, especially kelp, that has been left from a previous tide. Never walk on kelp since it has a slippery surface.

A tide table is important for planning your beach hike since portions of the beach trail may be blocked at high tide. It is best to hike the outgoing tide and allow plenty of time to reach any critical rounding point before the high tide. If the hike is to be a down and back trip, always plan on the prevailing wind blowing head-on for the initial leg so that the return trip will have a tail wind. High winds with a full pack can cause problems.

Small fresh water streams will generally spread out across a flat beach so that the hiker readily can cross them. Larger streams will require wading. The easiest crossing is midway to the ocean edge where your footing is firmer. Watch for new sand banks of coarser sand especially along larger streams. The footing here is deceptively dangerous.

The beach trail may be interrupted with rock outcroppings. There are often good foot and hand holds. By using caution, these outcroppings can be traversed. Sometimes an inspection of a sheer steep rock, even a relatively low one, will prove it to be impassable. This requires hiking over and around the headland. From Oregon north this means breaking trail through thick salal, Oregon grape, scrub spruce and other shore growth unless you happen on a game trail. On Vancouver Island, for example, this can resemble a jungle-like region so thick that you might have to go inland a bit to remain heading in your intended direction. Some headlands may have their own trails, for which we can thank earlier Indians and their travels.

While hiking a beach trail that requires climbing across stacked driftwood, be extremely cautious. The logs may not be secure, and they may throw you. Even without a pack one must be careful. Most ocean driftwood contains a thin and almost transparent layer of growth that is, when wet, slippery beyond imagination, lug boots or none. Ocean drift also is made of timbers, planks and dimension lumber, which often contains nails. Always be suspicious then, of a nice, long and flat plank.

Beach backpacking often requires covering a specific number of miles to reach a known destination in time to make camp for the night. It is best to set up your tent well beyond the high tide line. Here is better protection from the wind, which is customarily blowing from the sea. Pick a campsite where there is plenty of driftwood. Because of tides, currents and winds, not every beach will hold the drift. Beach drift will provide wood for the camp fire, seat and table space for cooking and eating and beachcombing relaxation. Be sure to adhere to local regulations regarding beach fires.

Once you have set up camp the casual beach meandering and beachcombing can be pure delight. There are the many wonders of tidal shore life to enjoy. Overhead is the quiet rustle in the trees. In the surf, a seal might be seen. Shorebirds and waterfowl provide company. Deer, raccoon and other wildlife will visit the beach to feed. Shells, agates and many other seashore items are readily available to examine.

In the driftwood there is also a vast array of man-made objects of oriental origin. These are continuously being deposited on our Pacific Ocean shores and are stashed away within the drift by the tides and wind. Japanese fishing gear, saki bottles, Chinese baskets, boxes with oriental markings, bamboo poles (which make excellent walking aids), shipwreck materials and plastic containers with Russian and Korean printed labels are typical items in the drift along a flat exposed beach. The prize most sought after is Japanese glass float. When this is found, the hiker always manages to find space in his pack even if the glass is of basketball size.

One final word about hiking an open coastal shoreline of the Pacific Ocean. The continuous pounding surf can almost always be heard. This steady roar is both pleasant and satisfying. Even after a period of offshore winds, the surf has a reassuring and quiet sound. If while you are walking along the sound of the surf suddenly stops and the ocean appears to be backing out away from the tide line, run for high ground. A sneaker wave is being formed. The wave first will appear to retreat and then will build with considerable force. It will pass up over the highest tide line at the beach bank at the elevation where bleached silver tinted driftwood may be rotting with moss. Many Pacific Northwest ocean beaches may be 800 feet wide at low tide, so a lot of ground might have to be covered in a hurry.

Catherine McNeill is happy upon finding her first Japanese glass fishing float. She beachcombed it on Olympic National Park Beach in Washington and had to carry it out 7 miles.
Phillipe de Faye photo

These erratic junior-grade tidal waves arrive at no known schedule. The warning signs must be obeyed if you are to escape a dunking, or worse, be carried out to sea. Among agate hunters who like to work the ocean gravel beds during the lowest tides of the year, there is an old adage that one never turns his back to the surf. Should you be hiking a beach that had a recent sneaker wave, be prepared for the possibility of dangerous aftermath. Large boom logs may be left teetering in jackstraw fashion. The slightest push may force a log to roll and cause an accident.

It is hard to equal the pleasures of a hike on a secluded outer beach with the surf on one side, sandpipers ahead and lush evergreens on the other. An eagle may soar overhead or an occasional osprey might dive into the surf for sea perch and fly away to feed its young. The edge of the Pacific Ocean is ever appealing to the hiker and little else quite matches the peaceful solitude that can be found there.

4 Northern California

Only a small portion of California is discussed here, approximately one-thirtieth of the state's area. This postage stamp-sized region is mostly mountainous, and fully 80 percent of the area is within the Klamath National Forest and Marble Mountain Wilderness. Here the potential for hiking is good. The population density of this region is low, so only a few of the state's 21 million people live or vacation here. In late August we had many of the trails to ourselves.

What first caught our attention was the dry climate and the unusual mountain formations. We were advised that there were rattlesnakes, but none rattled our way. There also was a lack of wind. The quiet of the trail was interrupted solely by an occasional bird's cry.

There are a variety of trails. Many are former logging roads. Some range from the freshly cut to those almost overgrown abound with saplings and blackberries. Other trails are so faint that, if the destination can't be sighted, it is doubtful where to proceed. Well-worn trails can terminate abruptly in a berry patch. Some game trails lead only to a watering spot. Sometimes a trail is just a scramble up a hillside to reach the top.

The Mount Shasta region is the southern most boundary of our Pacific Northwest hiking region. North of here the Klamath and Siskiyou Mountains do not conform to state boundaries. There are spectacular trails in wilderness areas of the Marble Mountains and Trinity Alps. Thompson Peak, 50 miles southwest from Shasta, has a glacier on its north slope. Many scenic areas can be visited and unusual vistas abound here. Numerous alluring trails attract the weekend hiker.

Toward the coast, lush vegetation extends from the flat river valley agricultural lands up into the foothills. Many upland lakes are available and may be enjoyed during an afternoon's hike. We hiked to one of these typical scenic spots, Taylor Lake, 30 miles southwest of Yreka and the Fort Jones neighborhood. We found this to be an easy afternoon family hike and had good camping.

We hiked the beautiful Castle Crags region southwest of Dunsmuir and tried the Seven Lakes Basin hoping to see the abandoned Ruby

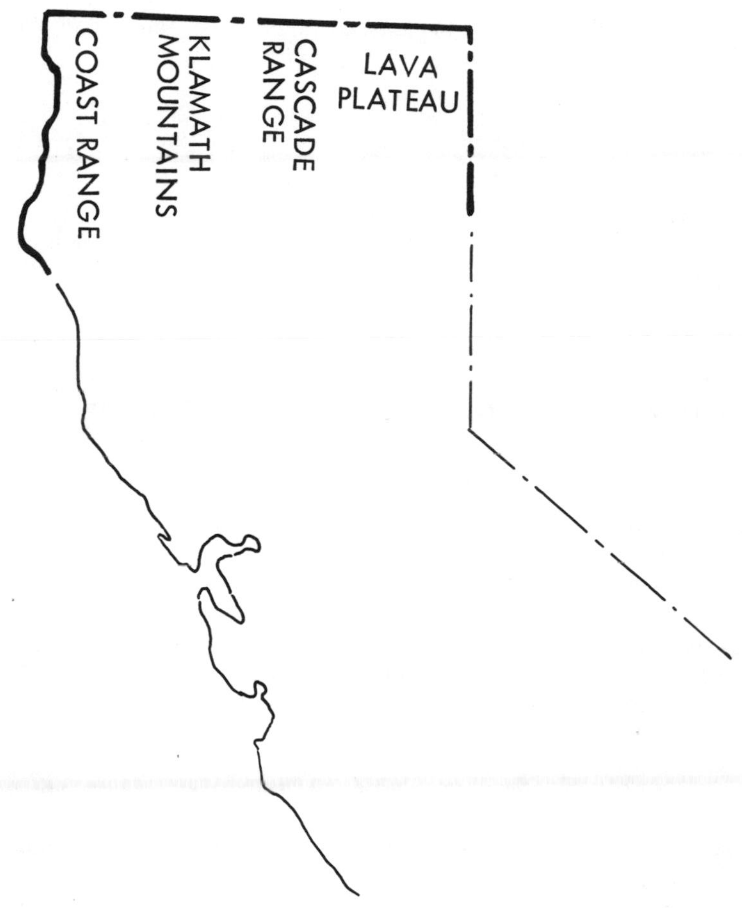

NORTHERN CALIFORNIA

Pearl Mine remains. However, we got lost in the underbrush and had to stop—but we will try again.

Near the Oregon border, in the region of Pyramid Peak north of Seiad, there are several excellent one-day and overnight hikes. Several of these are approached from the Oregon side via Medford. On the Pacific Ocean front we hiked the beaches both north and south of Crescent City to check ocean trail conditions.

South of Mount Shasta, beyond our arbitrarily imposed boundary, we leave the well-traveled trails of the Lassen Peak, Lake Tahoe and Yosemite areas for others to enjoy.

BLACK BUTTE - an extraordinary photographic platform for Mount Shasta.

One Way: 2½ miles; allow two hours one way.
High point: 6325 feet. *Elevation gain:* 1835 feet. Open clear, very little underbrush.
Open June through October.

Seldom does the hiker find a built-in, volcanic rock "tripod" that is 1800 feet high and set perfectly in front of a 14,000-foot snow-capped mountain for his picture taking. Black Butte is exactly that. This three-pinnacled "cinder cone" is almost within spitting distance of California's Mount Shasta. That is why Black Butte is a must for the northwest hiker.

Black Butte provides at its peak an ideal place for the hiker-photographer to catch Mount Shasta in her best northeast profile. Because Black Butte rises suddenly from the flat valley floor near Weed, California, it is a climbing hike.

Black Butte has been properly named. A mass of small shadows projects from its many individual rock faces and results in a dark appearance on the surface, even on a sunny day.

The butte is not a large pile of cinders or pumice but is solid rock. At the start of the trail the rocks will average the size of a football, but the higher you go the bigger the rocks get. Thus, hiking boots are a must. Only in a few places will the imprint of Vibram soles be seen along this trail. It is a good trail to practice the old hiking adage about stepping across the bigger rocks, not up on top of each one.

The trail begins at the northeast base of the butte and rises with an even, moderate grade. The first quarter-mile is in the woods, but it turns suddenly to open rocky hillside trail and stays that way to the top. Initially the trail heads west along the north face and presents an ever increasing number of fine vistas of Mount Shasta. It then follows south along the west face.

At about 1000 feet above the valley, the low rumble of a Southern Pacific switch engine and the occasional bleep of its air horn can

Mount Shasta as seen to the right from Interstate Highway 5 while approaching Black Butte from the south.

Author photo

clearly be heard almost directly below. Immediately adjacent to the railroad is multi-laned Interstate 5, with cars crawling along like so many ants on its cream-colored ribbon surface—all in marked contrast to the surrounding greenery. I had the feeling that if one of the stones I was standing on had started to roll, it might have gone all the way down and hit a freight car and then bounced right across the highway.

The trail abruptly turns east through the valley of the boulders. From here hawks may be seen soaring below. After a short distance there is a series of switchbacks before the trail heads west again above the depression that separates the two principal peaks. After a few more short switchbacks, you can see the top. Toward the top are fallen telegraph poles and line, remains of the former communication link with the lookout station. A few alpine firs eke out an existence just above them.

The achievement of having climbed the 1800-foot rock tripod and taking pictures of that beautiful chunk of mountain to the northeast was realized. Mt. Shasta seemed almost within reaching distance, but just far enough away to fit in the view finder. We took our pictures just in time: a vapor trail from a northbound jet overhead started to drift toward the peak and would have detracted from its magestic isolation that afternoon.

The lookout station has been removed but a small concrete foundation remains on the pinnacle. Conveniently enough, the lookout's small, auxiliary structure still stands—an extremely rustic cubicle perched precariously to the lee, over huge sloping slabs of rock. There is flat space near the lookout foundation where a few sleeping bags could be stretched out by those who might want to camp overnight.

There is no water on the butte, so a canteen is required. At rest stops sweetened iced tea is welcome. At the top Elaine pleasantly surprised me when she pulled out of her jacket two apples from the sackful we had brought from Mercer Island. Ski jackets are ideal garb for this late-summer hike. At this altitude there is usually the cool, steady afternoon breeze experienced in many mountain regions.

Whether it was beachcomber instinct or a desire to help clean up the pinnacle, we carried out a tea kettle lid. This apparently had been blown away and left behind when the lookout was torn down. This souvenir now hangs temporarily on the wall of my study, should any former lookout resident desire to claim it.

On the return trip, at one place the angle of the afternoon sun matched the sloping side of the butte, so our shadows were cast the full length down the face to about 3000 feet. All the way back are new vistas of Mount Shasta, some with trees as foreground frames.

Flora on the trail included windblown short-needle pine, Indian paintbrush and fireweed. Every once in a while the salubrious smell of an alpine bush alone made the hike worthwhile. Fauna we saw were hawks, mountain jays and slate gray salamanders.

To get to Black Butte, drive north on Interstate 5 from Redding, past the Shasta Lake recreational area (Dunsmuir) and on to Weed. Soon after Dunsmuir, Mount Shasta appears ahead to the right. Cone-shaped Black Butte is seen directly ahead. Interstate 5 skirts the base by the width of a pasture field and train tracks. The Butte is almost as impressive as Mount Shasta.

Take the South Weed Boulevard Exit and turn right, or east, at the exit stop sign. Continue one-tenth mile to the second stop sign, at Tee intersection. Turn right, or south, and proceed about one-half mile and turn left, east, past several abandoned buildings. Go about one-fourth mile to the Southern Pacific Railroad tracks and turn left. In a short distance take the ramp up to the right, opposite the salvage yard and cross the tracks. Then turn right, or south, at a water tank that is painted black. Drive parallel to the east-bound tracks. At four-tenths mile from the water tank, turn left into the side road that comes down to the tracks. Keep to the left again when that road forks. Keep to the left a third time. At two and six-tenths miles from the water tank you will encounter a junction that has power lines crossing diagonally overhead. Turn right and proceed onto this narrow road for about one-half mile, to a turnaround passable only by all-terrain vehicles—preferably bulldozers. Park here. The trail begins at the south edge of the turnaround. There are no markers anywhere.

Black Butte makes for a dandy morning or afternoon hike, particularly if you want to get to know Mount Shasta from its nearest friendly neighbor.

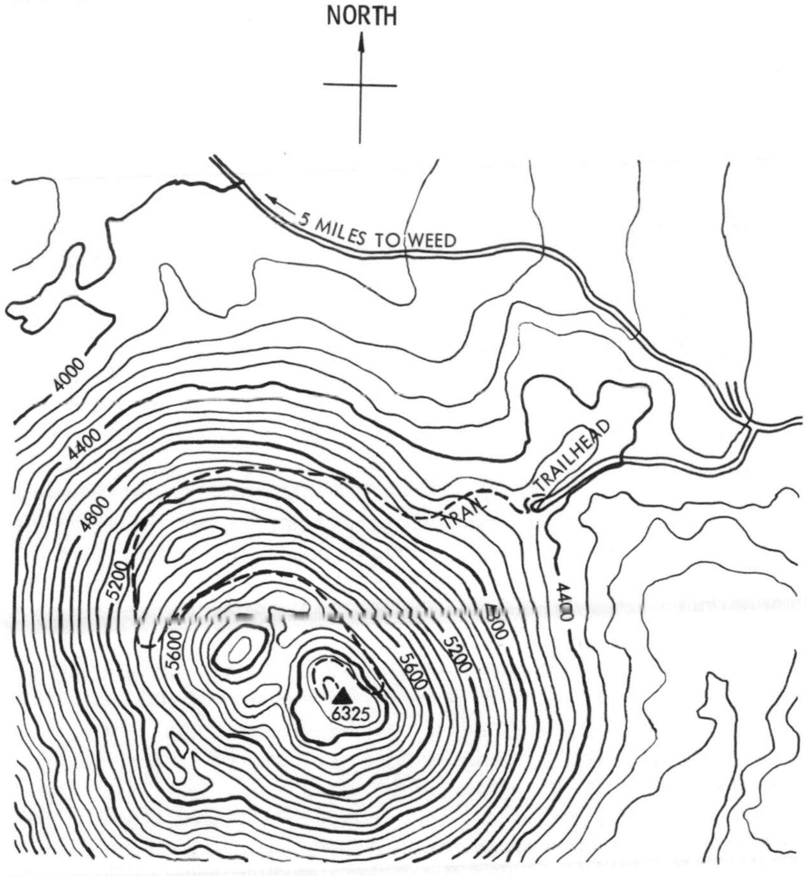

Black Butte

5 Oregon

It is conservatively estimated that between 1850 and 1875 more than 50,000 pioneers came over the Oregon Trail by covered wagon to settle in the lengthy Willamette Valley region. The pleasantly mild climate of the region that was a strong inducement to the pioneers encourages an exceedingly high percentage of the state's two million people, perhaps as many as 200,000, to take to the hills in pursuit of outdoor hiking pleasures. Consequently, the thousands of miles of trails now available throughout the state provide continuing incentives to new generations of hiking enthusiasts.

Oregon has an exciting variety of and striking contrasts in its trails. Within a day's drive, you can hike part of snowcapped Mount Hood, beach hike the edge of the sea to a Pacific Ocean sunset or walk the lava sands of sage brush dotted deserts.

Oregon has three mountain ranges—the Coast Range, the Cascades and the Blue Mountains all running north and south. They divide the state into four strips—the coast, the Willamette Valley, the barren central portion and the agricultural northeast.

The Cascades give Oregon's mild climate two general types of weather. The western half has lush growth, forests and fertile valleys with approximately 50 inches of annual rainfall. The eastern side has drier conditions with the rainfall averaging less than one third as much. In the south central region is the Great Sandy Desert with shifting sand dunes, dry lakes and lava beds.

The fauna in the Oregon Cascades includes the conies, marmots and deer. Coyotes and bears occasionally are seen. Sections of Oregon have poison oak and ticks, so prepare for them. Rattlesnakes dwell on the east side of the Cascades, so precautions should be taken when hiking dry hot rock ledges.

There are many separate hiking regions in Oregon. The Siskiyou Forest and Crater Lake region along with the central Cascade regions of the Umpqua, Rogue River, Deschutes and Willamette National Forests are just a few. The Blue Mountain region, Wallawa Mountains, Malheur Lake, Steens Mountains, Hart Mountain Refuge and Three Sis-

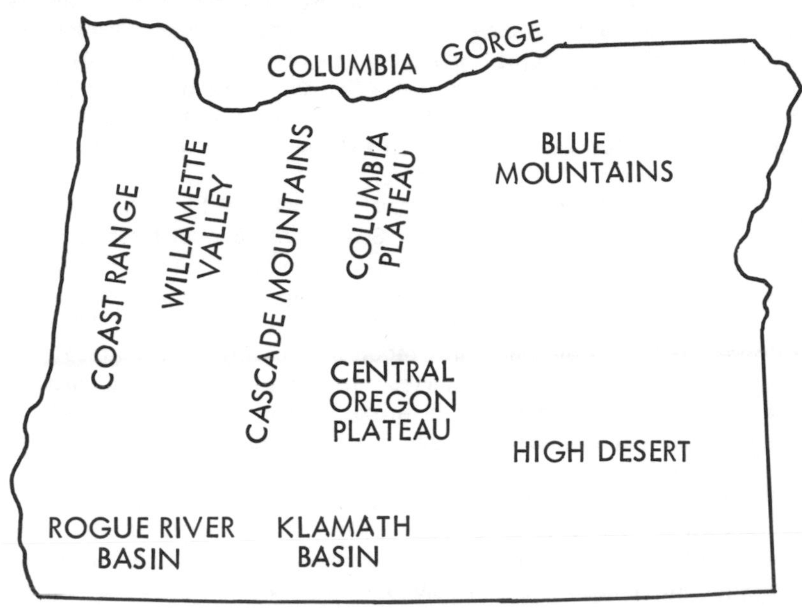

OREGON

ters area are some others. All of these are favorite haunts for local hikers who make it a point to hike a certain trail once every year.

In the Mount Hood area alone, for example, there are 800 miles of trails. Abundant wildflowers, including rhododendrons and carpets of flowers at different elevations make the area a veritable paradise.

The coastline is a favorite place to hike. Oregon has over 350 miles of beautiful sandy shoreline. Most of the beaches are readily accessible and can be hiked all year. The sand dunes, rocky cliffs and wide flat sandy beaches encased by nearby mountains fascinate all who visit here. The ever changing moods of the Pacific Ocean add to the variety. Oregon probably has more hikers who beachcomb and beachcombers who hike than any other state.

The Oregon Cascades generally are covered with national parks and forests; thus, there are many choices for hiking, backpacking and camping. It is no surprise that numerous hiking organizations flourish in the state.

Four National Park service areas have been established in Oregon. Crater Lake National Park is accessible all year and features camping, nature walks, boat rides and a museum. The crater rim drive is clockwise around the lake. The Oregon Caves National Monument features guided walks through the caves all year. Fort Clatsop National Memorial has an interpretive center and a replica of the fort that Lewis and Clark built to spend the winter of 1805-1806. Here are the restored trails they used for exploration and hunting. The fourth is the Oregon Dunes National Recreational Area, an extensive sand dune strip about 20 miles long north of Winchester Bay.

About one fourth of the state consists of national forest lands. Here the U.S. Forest Service administers 13 different national forests. Some 565 Forest Service campgrounds provide almost 10,000 tent, trailer and picnic sites. The Bureau of Land Management provides another 1300 campsites and picnic units for activities including hiking.

There are more state parks in Oregon than in any other state. Roadside rest areas and public campsites cater to all travelers. Regardless of which section you choose to hike, parks always are found easily. A number of smaller recreational sites are located in the more remote sections of the state.

The state maintains some 233 parks, waysides and recreational areas. State park campsites now are so much in demand that they are on the reservation system. Reservations by telephone, letter or in person are required. A campsite information center at Salem has current information on campsite availability. The toll free number, 1-800-452-0294, is available weekdays, May 15 through early September, for such information. Further guidance can be obtained by writing State Parks and Recreation Section, 525 Trade Street, Salem, Oregon 97310.

In addition to the state parks, there are 300 county parks with over 5500 picnic units and campsites available for a wide variety of activities including picnicing, sightseeing and nature stury.

Over 50 public recreation sites have been provided by private power and timber corporations, including some 1150 picnic and campsites that are also available to the hiker.

The tally of all the national, state, county and private parks and recreational areas proves that you will find some recreational site every few miles in almost checkerboard fashion across the entire state especially west of the Cascades. Thus with the mild climate, plentiful facilities and a variety of geography to behold, it is only natural that the Oregon hiker leaves footprints on his favorite trails.

Oregon State Coast Trail

A lesser known north-south trail is the Oregon State Coast Trail, which ultimately stretches the entire beach length of the state. In 1915 the 400 mile Oregon coastline was set aside for public use. With the passage of the Recreational Trails Act of 1971, Federal money made it possible for this trail to be officially designated.

The first portion of the coastline to receive designation as part of the

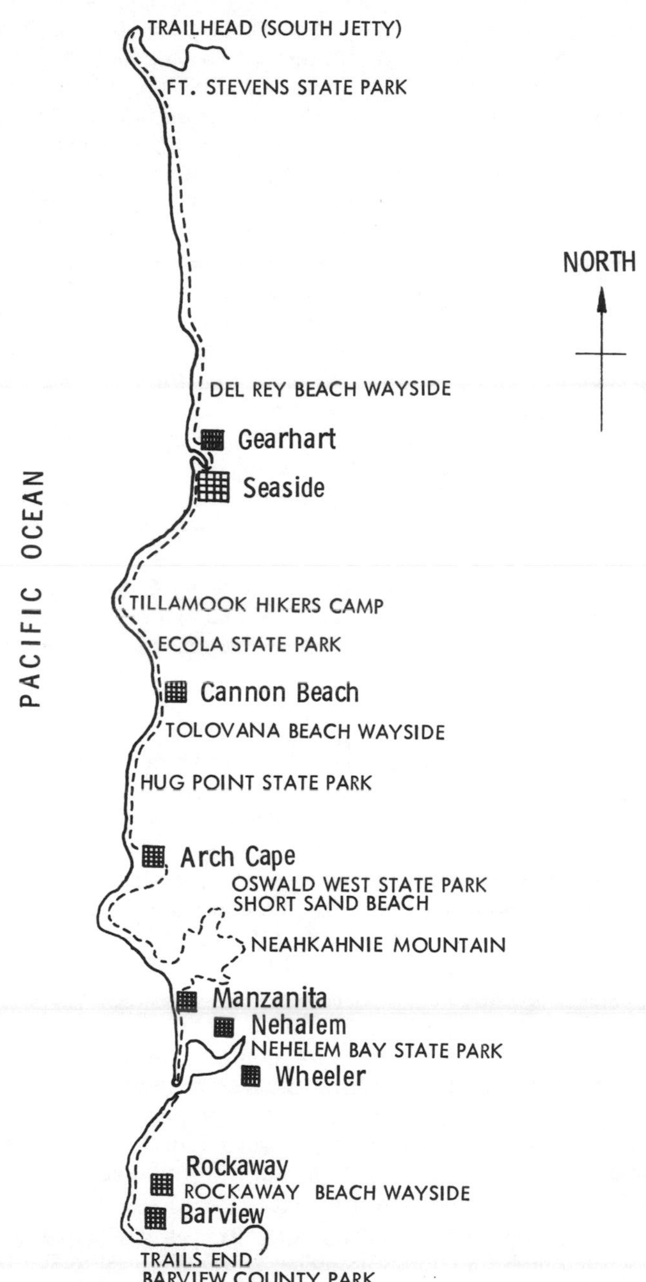

Oregon Coast Trail

Oregon State Coast Trail was the 32 miles of existing trails of Cape Lookout, Ecola Beach, Oswald West and Saddle Mountain. An advisory council has given top priority to the ocean coastline stretches because it has some of the most strikingly beautiful vistas on the Pacific Coast.

Early in 1976 a section approximately 62 miles, between the Columbia River and Tillamook Bay, was added to this trail system. This portion starts at the South Jetty of the Columbia River. The jetty is the largest harbor control project attempted by the U.S. Army Corps of Engineers. It consists of hugh rock blocks extending about four miles into the Pacific Ocean: and, in company with a north jetty on the Washington side of the Columbia, provides a channel for Columbia River traffic. The cross section of the South Jetty is about 80 feet wide and 40 feet high. Just south of the jetty, Fort Stevens State Park can be found in whose confines lies the beach wreck of the *Peter Iredale,* a large sailing ship which was driven ashore in 1906. Every year she attracts thousands of visitors and probably has been the subject of more photographers and artists than any other shipwreck along the Pacific.

Further south fifteen miles, the beach trail goes inland approximately three miles to Gearhart and back out again to the coast at Seaside. Here we can pick up the Lewis and Clark trail of 1805 and inspect, in Seaside, a replica of the salt cairn that the expedition used. Sea water was boiled to extract the salt for the preservation of meat to be eaten on their return eastbound journey across the wilds of the Louisiana Purchase.

Just south of Seaside we head up the Ecola State beach trail on Tillamook Head. From here Tillamook Rock, with its abandoned lighthouse, is seen about a mile offshore. This area has broad sandy beaches, Sitka spruce, bird rookeries, intertidal zones rich in marine life, driftwood, gulls, ducks and sandpipers, waving swordgrass, sand dunes, shells and wind shaped trees.

From Tillamook Head the trail goes through Cannon Beach, Tolovana Beach Wayside and Hug Point State Park. At Arch Cape it goes east across town to Oswald West State Park, named for the governor who set aside the Oregon coastline for public use. Past Short Sand Beach the trail again goes inland for four miles over Neahkahnie Mountain, the locale of numerous treasure hunters, and then beachward through Manzanita and Nehalem Bay State Park. Here it must be decided whether to hike south on the spit after having made arrangements to get ferried across from the south tip or to hike around the bay on the highway shoulder. It is well worth the trouble to arrange for private transportation across the river.

From here it is seven miles past Rockaway to Barview County Park, where the trail currently ends. It is believed that the rest of the Oregon State Coast Trail will be designated, marked and mapped by 1984.

The trail incorporates four public campgrounds: Fort Stevens State Park, Oswald West State Park, Nehalem Bay State Park and Barview

County Park. Two primitive campsites are being considered at Tillamook Head and at a point near Hug Point. Cannon Beach offers both private campground and youth hostel. Motel accommodations are available along the route.

A beachcomber-hiking friend of mine from Coos Bay set out to walk the entire coast of Oregon, section by section. He is about 80 percent finished, done in his spare time over three years. To my knowledge, no hiker has walked the entire coastal route.

ANGORA PEAK - a trail up a mountain named for a hiking club.

Round trip: 8 miles; allow one day.
High point: 2775 feet. Elevation gain: 2575 feet. Easy, with moderate underbrush.
Open February to November.

Most outdoor clubs are named for a region or mountain, but have you ever heard of a case where a mountain was named for a hiking club? Angora Peak in Oregon is one of those rare instances, so named after the Angora Hiking Club of Astoria, Oregon.

The Angora Hiking Club was founded atop Saddle Mountain on July 4, 1920. About 10 years later the club corresponded with the state geographic board regarding the naming of the peak, which has been so designated on maps since that time.

This 2800-foot high peak in southern Clatsop County invites all lovers of the outdoors to another challenge—a trail heading inland yet near to the Pacific Ocean. This trail appeals to the hiker because it is impassable for automobile traffic, although it probably was once a logging road. It is wide in most places, but much of the surface consists of cobblestone-size rocks. Thus your boots will be put to good use. Washouts are prevalent, as would be expected where mountain streams are continually testing water-course drainage routes.

The trail initially is gradual but steepens towards the objective with increasing rock outcroppings. However the view improves and several fine vistas are presented—the northern view is especially impressive.

Angora Peak has her seasonal moods and these changes are readily seen from and along the trail. At about the 2000-foot level is a flat plateau named "The Sled" by club members, after the remnants of a former logging outfit on skids. This spot provides a convenient stop for lunch with impressive three-directional views, including the seacoast three miles to the west. Ships at sea can be seen from here and coastal shoreline geography is discernible.

After lunch the trail ascends gradually with a good southerly view. The peak itself is seen after rounding a ravine. Here the road ends. There is no definite trail to the summit. For the final assault one makes his way through underbrush, around stumps and on logs.

Once on top there is a spectacular view in all directions. Within a

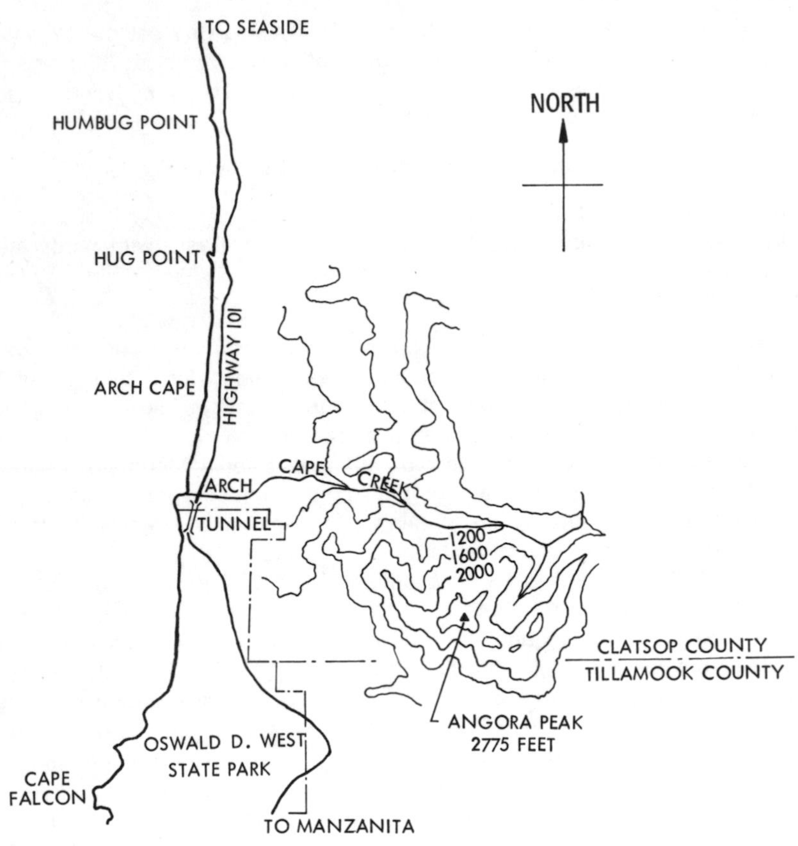
TO SEASIDE
NORTH
HUMBUG POINT
HUG POINT
HIGHWAY 101
ARCH CAPE
CAPE
ARCH
CREEK
TUNNEL
1200
1600
2000
CLATSOP COUNTY
TILLAMOOK COUNTY
ANGORA PEAK
2775 FEET
OSWALD D. WEST
STATE PARK
CAPE
FALCON
TO MANZANITA

Angora Peak

Gate at end of Arch Cape Hill Road is entrance of trail leading to Angora Peak in northwest Oregon.
Author photo

45-degree arc starting in the northeast are four snow-capped mountains, all rising majestically to between 10,000 and 14,000 feet—Mount Rainier, St. Helens, Adams and Hood in that order. Directly north are such lesser prominences as Onion Peak, Sugarloaf and Saddle Mountains, all named for their obvious shapes. On an extremely clear day, parts of the Columbia River may be seen 30 miles to the north.

Be prepared to be vulnerable to the weather of the particular day at that altitude. In most seasons there will be strong winds. When there are low clouds or coastal fog, the ascent into bright, clear sunshine is a special treat. This peak is generally snow-free from February to November. However, the capriciousness of Pacific Ocean storms may alter the norm.

Expect to see the usual deer and elk; bear and cougar have also been reported along this coastal range region. The flora consists of numerous varieties of wildflowers, hillside grasses and alpine ground coverings, all providing a serene setting and an ideal one-day contrast to wherever we call home.

How can you get there? Starting from Portland, drive 76 miles northwest on Highway 26 to the coast and turn left, or south, onto Highway 101. Drive south about 10 miles past Cannon Beach, to Tolovana Park and Arch Cape. Upon approaching the Arch Cape tunnel, turn left, or east, onto a country road that parallels Arch Cape Creek. The trail begins at the end of this road, about one-half mile in from the highway. The peak can be seen along the highway while approaching this turnoff.

CAPE LOOKOUT - the rocky peninsula that extends into the Pacific.

One way: Two and one-half miles; allow two hours one way.
High point at start: 800 feet.
Elevation at Look out: 500 feet.
Easy day trip.
Open year-around.

The significance of this trail is its location on a high rocky peninsula that extends several miles from the shore out into the Pacific Ocean. A similar view does not exist anywhere else along the Pacific. From this cape's view the northbound spring migration of grey whales can be seen as well as the south migration in the fall. Often the whales come within a few hundred yards of the cape.

Cape Lookout is well-named. This massive headland juts seaward like an irresistible rock finger from a coast that, on both sides, has a wide flat sandy shoreline. This formidable peninsula has steep rocky sides that extend directly into the water. Thus this is the beach in this area that has a fortress-like profile.

The trail is found in the Cape Lookout State Park. The trailhead begins at a high inland point with a parking area on the coast road that connects Tillamook and Sand Lake. At this point there is a commanding view of the Pacific Ocean. The trail initially winds through a dense spruce stand along the south side of the peninsula. At about one-quarter mile is a commemorative plaque on the right, at shoulder level, denoting the site of an Army Air Force aircraft accident in 1943. Some of the larger pieces of the wreckage may be seen in the underbrush west of the plaque. The trial skirts a steep drop to the water 600 feet below.

The trail heads westward. At about the one-mile point, it crosses over to the north side to a side trail view with a northwestern exposure. The trail threads another one and one-half miles to the final view at the southwest corner of the Cape, but it is muddy much of the time. On a clear day Tillamook Head can be seen 42 miles to the north and Cape Foulweather 39 miles to the south. A whistler buoy is located about a quarter mile offshore, where inside grey whales occasionally are seen.

Plan for rain and fog. However, an old coastal adage says that at least some part of everyday will be clear. It may occur at night, but it could be during the day. We experienced clear weather over half of the time during some dozen visits in every season.

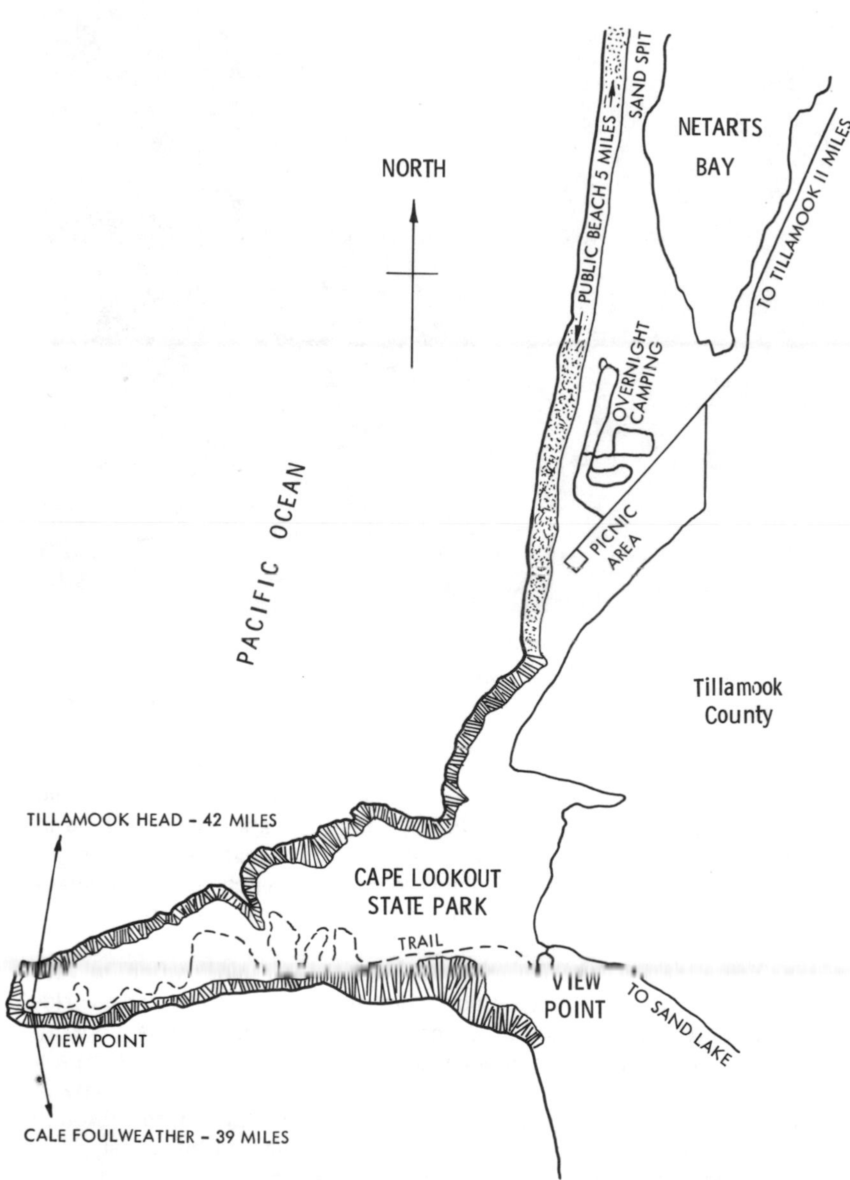

Cape Lookout

Entrance sign points to view point and parking lot to Cape Lookout trail.

Author photo

Cape Lookout is perhaps the most scenic headland on the Pacific Coast. It was set aside as a rain forest wilderness and wildlife refuge in 1935. This 2000 acre state park also includes extensive overnight camping, picnic and bathing facilities located at beach elevation immediately north of the cape itself. These conveniences are especially attractive to the hiker traveling here from a considerable distance.

The park has a special attraction for hikers, bird watchers and beach walkers. Over 150 species of bird life have been recorded. Numerous shorebirds and waterfowl can be seen around Cape Lookout since they nest in the rugged walls of this headland. North of the park bordering Netarts Bay are marshes that provide a haven for a variety of birds and other life indigenous to this area. The trail passes through growths of spruce, hemlock and other species native to the coast.

To get to Cape Lookout from Portland drive west on State Route 26 for 26 miles to the interchange onto Route 6. Here go 13 miles to Glenwood then 36 miles to Tillamook. Drive west out of Tillamook to the Cape Lookout-Cape Meares junction. Turn left and follow Cape Lookout signs for 11 miles. Upon entering the park, take Sand Lake

At day's end weary hikers approach overnight campground at Cape Lookout State Park. Broad flat sandy beaches of the Oregon coast provide carefree hiking opportunities for outdoorspeople of all ages.

Thomas W. Ray photo

Because of the rugged and inaccessible terrain at Cape Lookout, several large pieces of World War II bomber wreckage still remain for hiker to examine.

Thomas W. Ray photo

Cape Lookout State Park peninsula trail as seen looking south. Park trail is near Tillamook, Oregon.
Burford Wilkerson photo

road, which diagonals left. This winds up to the top of the headland for about two and one-half miles to an 800 foot elevation summit where a prominent sign identifies Cape Trail parking to the right. The trailhead starts from this parking area.

Bring camera, binoculars and water. When viewing the Pacific Ocean from the west end of the trail, enjoy the bird life and grey whales in season. Remember that you are standing on a geographically significant area almost exactly on the 45th latitude, named by fur trader Captain John Meares in 1788.

KINGS MOUNTAIN — fire-devastated area that is successfully reforested.

One way: 2½ miles; allow two to three hours one way.
High point: 3226 feet.
Elevation gain: 2540 feet.
Mountainous terrain, 41 acres of roads making travel difficult.
Open March through December.

Kings Mountain

Perhaps America's most devastating forest fire took place in 1933 in northwestern Oregon between Portland and Tillamook. Known as the Tillamook Burn, more than 300,000 acres of prime timber growth in the heart of the Coastal Mountain range were lost.

Here is the story of the burn. Following weeks of dry weather with temperatures between 90 and 100 degrees, some 200 fires or varying size burned in Oregon forests that summer. On August 14, 1933, a logging operation fire started at Gales Creek bordering the east edge of this roadless, uninhabited forest area that extends between Portland and the Pacific coast — a distance of 60 miles. A hot, gusty east wind fanned the fire up a canyon. Burning debris started a second fire front 15 miles to the south. Within three days 1,800 men were involved in fighting this fire, which had spread along a 15-mile front.

On the tenth day the fire "blew up." Smoke clouds mushroomed to 40,000 feet; the fire line grew to 50 miles in length. Now the strong

King's Mountain seen in the distance from bank of Wilson River east of Tillamook, Oregon.
Author photo

east winds that had fed this holocaust caused airborne debris to fall on ships 500 miles at seas. Before long Pacific Ocean currents were carrying charred debris, two feet deep in places, back onto the beach.

Later the wind switched to the northwest and pushed portions of the 40-mile-wide smoke cloud as far as Reno, Nevada. On the 22nd day a pelting rain put a damper on the conflagration which, with two adjoining major fires at that time, had ravaged 600 square miles.

But all was not lost. Logging operations soon went into full swing to save the usable burned timber before it was lost to insects and rot. Because of the magnitude of this fire — plus three smaller fires in 1939, 1945 and 1951 — all within the original burn boundaries — salvage operations went on for 25 years.

This burn area now is within the Tillamook State Forest, where the results of man's reforestation and Mother Nature's effort to heal herself can be observed during a day-long hike.

To get to Kings Mountain drive east from Tillamook on State Route 6 for a distance of just over 25 miles. Much of this road follows Wilson River, a popular fishing, swimming and picnicking recreational area. Watch for the green and white vertical mile post signs along the way.

This two-foot high cedar survey post is an important trail identification marker. It is painted orange on the top and is found beyond the cleared grassy area about 200 yards in from State Highway 6.
Author photo

Past Jones Creek Forest Camp and at six mile past the 25-mile marker and where Wilson River is on your right (south) prepare to stop. Look for a 15-foot length of broken stonework masonry retaining wall eight feet high constructed on the left (north) side of the highway, at a road cut.

The trail begins about 200 feet west of this stonework and is identified by an unmarked six-foot-high, 15-inch thick log pylon on the left side of what formerly was a logging road entrance. A short stretch of this road provides out-of-sight, off-highway parking even though there is adequate parking on both sides of busily traveled State Route 6. The logging roadbed becomes impassable by car within a few hundred feet due to erratic erosion by the small stream at the left, plus felled alder trees farther on.

In years past the trail had been marked with splotches of orange paint sprayed on new alder growth at about shoulder height. Because these guide markers have weathered in the ensuing years, some kind soul has sprayed a few trees with red splotches, and he deserves our many thanks. But these also have faded. Consequently these guide markings must be diligently searched out from the shadows and darker

Near the beginning of the trail is this grassy clearing filled with common cowparsnip and common yarrow plant growth. First trail marker post is alder growth ahead.

Author photo

places of the trail.

From the felled alders the trail continues into a grassy clearing, where in summer grow common cowparsnips by the thousands. Continue a short distance past the clearing until you locate a two-foot-high, five-inch-square wooden post, originally painted orange but now faded—an official survey point. Turn to the left for a short distance and then to the right. Climb a fairly steep grade to a second, almost level, abandoned logging road. At this road turn left, or west, and follow it to an open shale rock bed where you turn right. Proceed uphill to a small ridge and onto the saddle. Turn left onto the ridge and follow the guide markings through snags and new growth to the summit. From here on a clear day are beautiful vistas in all directions, with conical-shaped Mount Saint Helens, round-domed Mount Adams and streaked Mount Hood all standing snow-capped to the east.

Each year in the late summer some good Samaritan or hiking group should undertake this hike with several cans of orange spray paint and retouch these four-inch-wide splotches. Without these trail guide markings one could soon become hopelessly lost. We found ourselves backtracking even though the trail was marked about every 100 yards. Fortunately some of the paint splotches had been added on the backside, and these assisted measurably in our return.

At one place we became lost because we mistakenly followed a deer trail; upon backtracking, we finally discovered a small piece of red ribbon tied to the twig of a 12-foot-high fir that had obliterated the trail. Whoever tied that red ribbon at that place deserves special commendation. In order to help anyone else in similar predicament, I placed three short tree limbs in the shape of an arrow at the start of the false trail. Perhaps the deer will see these and correct their route.

There is considerable new alder growth in the logging roadbeds. Behind and beyond the immediate alder and fir growth are burned stumps and charred logs, monuments of the fire, that now slowly rot to some unknown, long-term timetable. Along the trail are lupin, Oregon grape, daisy, foxglove and, occasionally, the rarer blue elderberry. New fir growth 30 feet high and two-foot-high seedlings are seen everywhere. Since the trail is mostly covered, it is cool and shaded—a welcome blessing on a hot August day. Mountain jays and other birds reminded us when returning to Tillamook to stop at the outstanding displays of wildlife at the Pioneer Museum there.

This trail is not readily visible much of the time because it is almost completely grown over with bracken, thimbleberry and five-inch-thick alder; apparently it is little used. The filtered sunshine through the trees would have provided perfect cover for any fawn that might have been standing alongside us as we hiked.

Reforestation efforts by the Oregon State Forestry Department and private industry have been most successful. The deer are back. Rabbits, squirrels and fish have been restocked, and bear and cougar are reported.

This hike is a very satisfying day trip. Here is the opportunity to see a new woodland being created, a veritable Phoenix from the ashes of catastrophes. Kings Mountain trail is a living interpretive display for the rebirth of our forest heritage.

LEWIS & CLARK — follow historic expedition's travels at Pacific Ocean.

One way: three separate portions totaling 6 miles; allow one day including car travel.
High point: Cape Disappointment, about 200 feet.
Elevation gain: primarily sea level hiking.
Good all year around weather permitting.

In 1805 President Jefferson sent Lewis and Clark west the length of the Louisiana Purchase to the Pacific to explore this vast territory and to lay claim to the lands in between. This expedition, consisting of 30 courageous explorers who traveled 8,000 miles on foot and by boat opened the way for other Americans to establish a foothold west of the Mississippi.

The final 500 mile leg of the westbound trek along the Columbia River to the Pacific Ocean was accomplished in dugout canoes, which they had hewed from ponderosa pine trees in Idaho beside the swift flowing Clearwater River.

On November 15, 1805, in the teeth of a winter ocean storm pounding away at the river mouth, the group landed their five dugouts on the north shore of the Columbia River, about eight miles short of the ocean edge. In heavy rain, wind, and without shelter they hiked out to Cape Disappointment, a rock protruding into the mouth of the Columbia. From here they went north to hunt for elk, retracing their steps. At the suggestion of the local Chinook Indians, they went across to the south shore of the river, where there was better hunting. There they built Fort Clatsop, named after the Indian tribe, for their wintering quarters in a protected inlet. They conducted hunting trips for food from this inlet.

Today it is still possible to retrace parts of this same route, even without a boat, thanks to the Astoria Toll Bridge, which now spans the mouth of the Columbia River. The avid Lewis and Clark enthusiast will want to follow this entire route by boat and by foot as those hearty pioneers did; however, with a combination of walking and driving several portions of the original route can be enjoyably hiked in one day.

The first portion of the trail begins on the north side of the Columbia River in the region of McGowan on Highway 101, two miles west of the Astoria Bridge. North of the highway is a small park containing a picnic site and an historic marker denoting the landing site of the Lewis and Clark expedition. Here we start. You will need a friend to drop you off and meet you along the way with your car.

Lewis and Clark

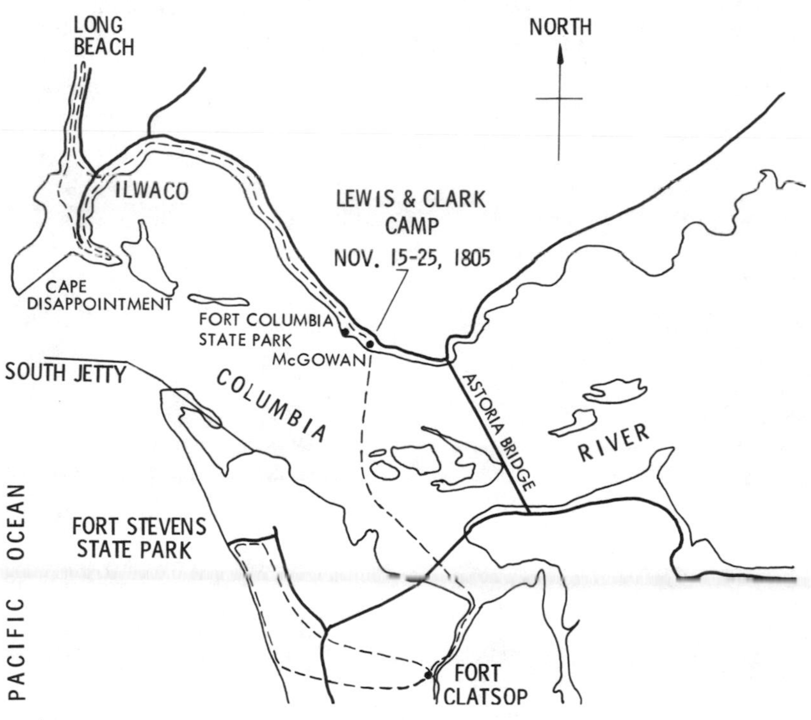

Salt cairn replica shows how Lewis and Clark boiled sea water for salt to preserve meat for return trip provisions from Pacific coast to St. Louis.
Author photo

Monument at McGowan on north side of the Columbia River marks campsite area of Lewis and Clark in 1805.

Author photo

Four mile long Astoria Bridge spans mouth of the Columbia RIver near where Lewis and Clark first viewed breakers of the Pacific Ocean in 1805.

Author photo

Trail sign at Fort Clatsop sets stage for hike to salt cairn built by Lewis and Clark in 1805 near Seaside, Oregon.

Author photo

Hike west one half mile alongside the road and through the tunnel, or if weather and tide permit, walk the beach which skirts a local rock outcropping—including the tunnel—to Fort Columbia State Park. The entrance is at the west end of the tunnel or at eight-tenth's mile. A stop at the park and visit to the interpretive center up the hill is well worth the time. Here are portrayed historical developments of the immediate region. Visiting hours are 10 a.m. to 4 p.m.

Now have your friend drive you west on Highway 101 past picturesque Chinook. At mile 7.1, immediately after crossing the Chinook River, stop at Stringtown Road on your left. Your friend can drive ahead on Highway 101 and pick you up, since Stringtown Road loops back to the highway in two miles. This loop road, running south of the main highway, borders the low river bank and follows through a representative area that Lewis and Clark took while hiking toward Cape Disappointment.

This country loop road is 2.8 miles in length and an easy walk. It is much too enjoyable to take by car. It passes by an occasional spruce and considerable scotch broom. Previous ocean storms have strewn driftwood into pastures here. The hiker will pass an occasional farm house. One was decorated with boom log ends.

We see poplar trees, old fences and even an airport. Wood is available at the river's edge for the cutting, driven ashore from prevailing southwest storms. The river mouth is four miles wide at this point and exposed to vagarities of the Pacific, as was experienced by the Lewis and Clark group.

This loop road joins the highway at about mile 9.1 where your friend is waiting. Then drive several miles to the town of Ilwaco. At the traffic light continue straight ahead another two miles to the Fort Canby entrance. Continue straight ahead to the recently completed Lewis and Clark Interpretive Center. A short walk from the parking lot to the right up the hill takes you to the old Fort Canby gun battery on Cape Disappointment and the interpretive center immediately beyond. To the south at the same elevation is the Cape Disappointment lighthouse.

Here you can view the Pacific Ocean, as Lewis and Clark did during their expedition, and also visit the interpretive center with displays covering their entire journey.

Lewis and Clark went north a few miles from here to the region now known as the town of Long Beach, and then returned to where they had landed at McGowan.

To follow in Lewis and Clark's footsteps on the south side of the Columbia River, you drive from Cape Disappointment east on highway 101 through Ilwaco, past Chinook, past Fort Columbia State Park to the Astoria Bridge. Here turn south onto the four mile lone bridge to Astoria. No pedestrians are allowed on the bridge. After paying the toll, turn right at the traffic light on Highway 101 and proceed about four miles across Youngs Bay causeway, to a left turn onto alternative Highway 101. In about two miles, the hiker will come to Fort Clatsop with its interpretive center, replica of the original fort and trails.

Because a continuous supply of food was all important to the expedition, hunting parties made forays for elk and deer meat. Such forays took them west from Fort Clatsop to the coast, and it is these footsteps we will follow.

Drive about eight miles west and north to Fort Stevens State Park with its beach areas. Park at the beach edge. Here the expedition hunters watched for the game to come down to the water's edge. On this same beach is the wreckage of the sailing vessel *Peter Iredale* which was driven ashore in 1906. From this well-known landmark we hike north toward the south jetty and then south for a few miles, as the Lewis and Clark hunters did, before turning eastward to Fort Clatsop. The solitude of this beach area with its ever extending line of driftwood is very impressive.

Hiking these brief portions of the trails used by the Lewis and Clark expedition members at the western end of their historic trek causes us to further appreciate the significance of their assigned task.

The effects of Pacific Ocean surf, tide, and storm are seen in the remains of British Bark ***Peter Iredale*** *wrecked in 1906.*

Author photo

To get to McGowan from Portland, Oregon, drive north on Interstate 5 about 45 miles to Kelso and turn west on State Route 4 for about 45 miles to Nacelle. Here, turn left on State Route 401, go for about 12 miles to the bridge and join Highway 101. Continue west on 101 for about two miles to a Lewis and Clark marker.

MARY'S PEAK - the most prominent peak in Oregon's Coast Mountains.

One way: half mile; allow one and one-half hours round trip.
High Point: 4097 feet.
Elevation gain: 350 feet.
Easy half-day climb.
Best time: April through October.

The historical and geographical significance of this trail is in overlooking the broad Willamette Valley region. This rich farmland of the Oregon Territory was the principal reason why families migrated, in wagon trains, to the Pacific Northwest. Good soil, water supply, plentiful game and opportunity all contributed to the pioneering spirit.

Mary's Peak

NORTH
TO ROCK CREEK ROAD
AND HIGHWAY 34
2500
2750
3000
3250
3500
CAMPGROUND
PARKING LOT
MARYS
PEAK
4097 FEET
MARYS PEAK ROAD
TO HIGHWAY 34 PARK ENTRANCE

Upon turning off Oregon State Highway 34, prominent entrance sign greets all visitors.

Author photo

The northwest view from Mary's Peak towards Wilamette River area as clouds descend to level with the peak. The Wilamette region was where many Oregon Trail pioneers settled.

Author photo

Mary's Peak, southwest of Corvalis, is one of the best known points in Western Oregon. It is the most prominent peak along the Oregon Coast Range, and ranks with the highest peaks of Oregon's extreme southwestern corner. Mary's Peak was apparently named for the nearby Mary's River, which got its name from: the name of the first white woman to cross this river in 1846, an early settler in memory of both his sister and wife who he murdered and/or early Hudson Bay French fur traders who dubbed it St. Mary's.

The trail to the peak, from the parking lot trailhead, is about one-half mile with an elevation gain of about 500 feet. It is an open, gravel surface, with no protection from the wind. There are washouts, rivulets and rocks along this trail. At the top is an abandoned lookout. Even from a distance its two-storied structure is impressive. Its sturdy construction attests to its having weathered the elements. A concrete communications bunker alongside defies change.

Expect to be at cloud level when visiting the peak. There is usually a wind, but it is not objectionable. Mary's Peak is only 25 miles from the Pacific Ocean, so the wind will have moisture in it.

Regarding fauna, we only saw two hawks. Otherwise we seemed to have the whole mountain to ourselves, a rarity nowadays. There is a wealth of flora: fireweed, spirea, goldenrod, vine maple, foxglove, pearly everlasting, daisies, lupine and lavendar elderberry.

Near tip of Mary's Peak this stand of alpine spruce provides serene setting for camping area.
Author photo

To get to Mary's Peak from Corvalis, head south for about one-half mile then turn right (west) on Route 20 towards Philomath, four miles distant. This is also Route 34. About one mile past Philomath, turn left on Route 34 heading southeast. At about nine miles watch for the right hand turn to the Siuslaw National Forest Recreation Area.

From the entrance follow a nine-mile paved road of easy grade winding through scenic stands of evergreen trees. Beautiful vistas open up as you continue into open alpine meadows.

Near these meadows, below the parking lot, is a beautiful campground in an unusual thicket of tall spruce. It has developed facilities and is ideal for those who would like to further explore the area.

For an alternate route to return to Philomath, take the woodsy road past watershed sign on the left and after five miles join with Griffin Creek. Turn right on Rock Creek Road to Route 34. Turn left (north), and five miles brings you to Philomath. Keep going on Route 20 to Corvalis.

This is an ideal hike for a family with small children. All will remember the mountains to the west and the Willamette Valley to the east. Bring camera and binoculars. Water is available.

NEAHKAHNIE MOUNTAIN - a Spanish Manila galleon's treasure is nearby.

One way: one mile; allow one hour one way.
High point: 1661 feet.
Elevation gain: 1010 feet.
Well-packed, well-traveled trail.
Easy afternoon walk.
Open all year-round.

In 1715 the Spanish Manila galleon *San Francisco Xavier* sailed from the Philippine Islands, bound for Acapulco, and was never heard of again. Now there is circumstantial evidence that she was probably shipwrecked during a storm on the Oregon coast near the foot of Neahkahnie Mountain, which juts prominently into the Pacific Ocean. Coastal Indian oral history indicates that treasure from this galleon was buried by members of the ship's company at the base of the mountain. In the nearby sand beaches beachcombers still find portions of candle-wax, a cargo also known to have been aboard that square-rigged sailing ship. On my desk is a piece of this wax that has been Carbon-14 dated to the approximate year of the ship's disappearance.

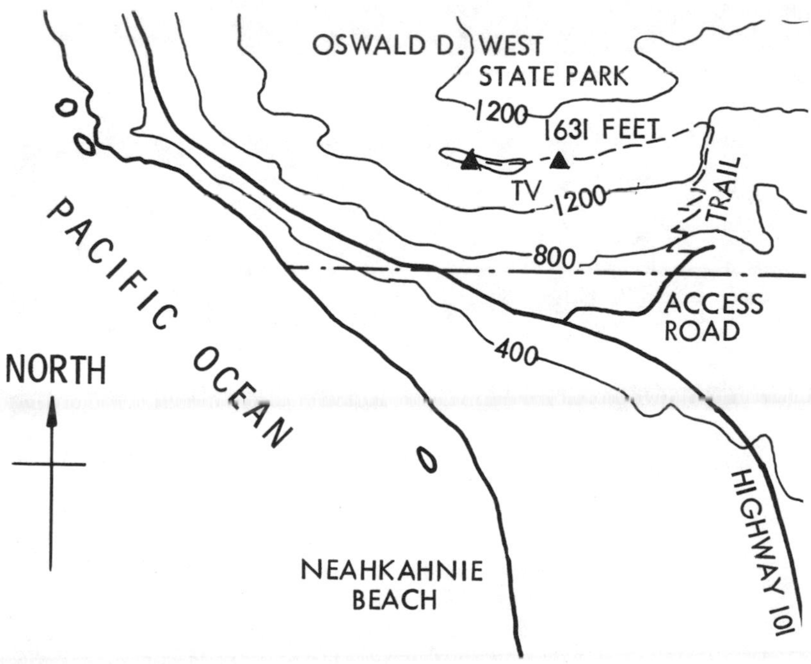

Neahkahnie Mountain

Burford Wilkerson displays piece of Spanish Manila galleon beeswax cargo where it was found in 1909 near Neahkahnie Mountain in Pacific Ocean beach sands. In 1961 he obtained a carbon-14 dating of this specimen confirming its approximate age to a galleon shipwreck in 1715. The wax resides in the Tillamook County Pioneer Museum, Tillamook, Oregon.

Arline Wilkerson photo

Scene looking up southern face of Mount Neahkahnie from trail parking lot. Trail begins about ½ mile in from highway.

Author photo

What more compelling invitation is needed to hike this mountain than knowing that buried somewhere near the trail may be a Spanish treasure chest filled with silver bars, gold coins and jewels?

To hike up this summit select any clear day; then sit and enjoy the magnificent view. Listen to the muffled but constant pounding of the ocean surf on wide, flat beaches 1661 feet directly below. The village of Neahkahnie Beach, the nearby golf course where in years past treasure hunters have dug unsuccessfully, U.S. Highway 101 and the Pacific coastline all match the topographic map—like the living three-dimensional model that it is. Only the occasional call of a bird or the far-away rumble of a truck on the highway below can be heard.

To get to Neahkahnie Mountain from Portland, drive northwest to coastal U.S. Highway 101—a distance of 76 miles. Turn left, or south, and drive about 18 miles to a readily discernible Neahkahnie Mountain Trail sign mounted on an eight-foot-high post at the left side of the road. At this marker turn left, or east, up a crushed rock road and drive one-half mile to the trail head, where there is adequate turnaround and parking.

The well-manicured trail begins at the trail marker with a series of switchbacks up the open, brush-covered southern face at a steady and

Mount Neahkahnie juts out into the Pacific Ocean as seen from the broad beaches at Nehalem Spit, Oregon. Note the swordgrass foothold which keep sand dunes from blowing away.

Author photo

even slope. About half-way it proceeds into a shaded, wooded area of spruce and hemlock with more gentle switchbacks up the southeastern edge of the mountain. Upon approaching an east-west ridge near the top, the trail joins a larger, crushed-rock access road. Here a six-foot-high timber marker post directs one to the left, or west, toward the summit. An abandoned television relay station is located to the right. Follow this new road west along the ridge to the site of the currently operating television relay station. Past this station the trail drops a bit but again continues up a very narrow ridge to a second summit a few hundred feet away. Here are breath-taking vistas in all directions.

Very near the summit wild rose, foxglove goatsbeard and thimbleberry can be seen along the trail. En route is salal and kinnikinnick. Most of the trail is well used, particularly on weekends, by hikers of all ages. Tennis shoes, shorts and a light jacket are satisfactory garb for a summer trip. There is no water on the mountain, so a filled canteen is handy.

It is easy to understand why those who live relatively nearby make repeated trips to this peak. The aesthetic rewards are many, including the opportunity to look down at the ocean, the beaches and the golf course—and to ponder where the *San Francisco Xavier* treasure might still be buried and what the circumstances really were of its deposit.

OREGON TRAIL BARLOW ROAD - a pioneer wagon trail.

One way: 133 miles; allow 9 days.
High point: 4155 feet at Barlow Pass.
Elevation at The Dalles: 98 feet.
Elevation at Oregon City: 55 feet.
All types of terrain: enjoyable series of separate hikes.
Open July through September.

The Oregon Trail covered wagon era had its beginnings in the 1830s. Earlier exploration to the Pacific Northwest by Lewis and Clark in 1805 and the John Jacob Astor fur-trading expeditions to the mouth of the Columbia River in 1811 opened the way.

By 1843 several wagon trains consisting of approximately 300 wagons had made it to The Dalles, Oregon, after starting from Independence, Missouri. The Dalles was considered the end of the overland Oregon Trail. To reach the broad rich agricultural lands of the Willamette River Valley, which reaches south from the Columbia River past Oregon City, for several hundred miles, there was a difficult, dangerous and costly 100-mile raft trip down the Columbia River rapids. To make this trip wagons had to be disassembled and put on rafts to make the treacherous river run. Many who managed the overland trek across the plains and mountains lost their lives during the final leg.

In 1845 Samuel Barlow with seven wagons and Joel Palmer with 23, reasoned that an alternate route, south and west around the base of Mount Hood, should be attempted. The William Rectōr party also joined in this venture. Using some Indian trails while carving a new route much of the way, they finally succeeded after great hardships. This new wagon route went south of Mount Hood across the Cascade Range. By fall of the following year 152 wagons had arrived at Oregon City over this road. The United States had become a two-ocean nation and history was made.

The Barlow Road, the final extension of the Oregon Trail, winds along for about 133 miles, generally away from highways. In about 68 miles, it rises to Barlow Pass, which has an elevation of 4155 feet, and then descends to Oregon City, another 65 miles.

To hike the entire Barlow Road would be a major undertaking since it is not a continuous path, but to do a little at a time would be an enviable achievement. It is predicted that a complete book for hiking this historic trail will be available in the near future. Don & Roberta Lowe, in *20 Hiking Trails, Northern Oregon Cascades,* mention the Pioneer Bridle Trail near Rhododendron follows small portions of the Barlow Road.

There now are approximately 20 historical markers along the Barlow Road thanks to past and continuing efforts of the Clackamas County and Wasco County Historical Societies as well as the U.S. Forest Service, D.A.R. chapters, the Sons and Daughters of Oregon Pioneers, the Pioneer Descendants and the Touch and Gro' Garden Club. The sever-

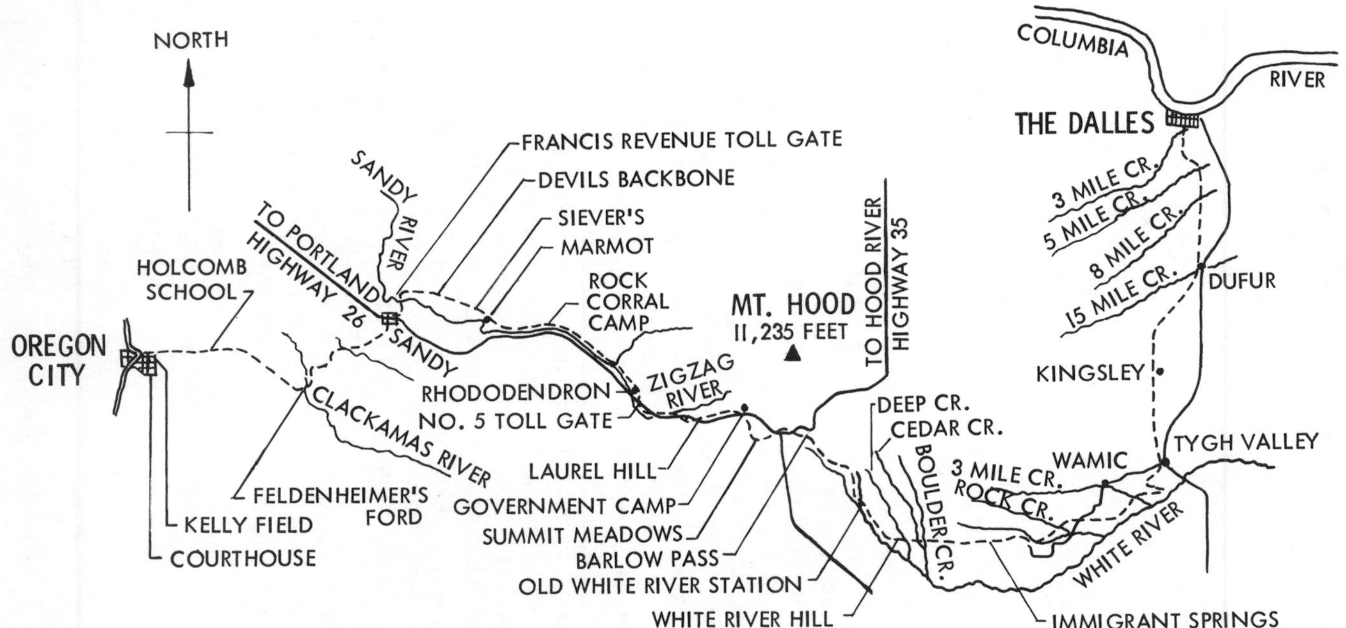

Oregon Trail Barlow Road

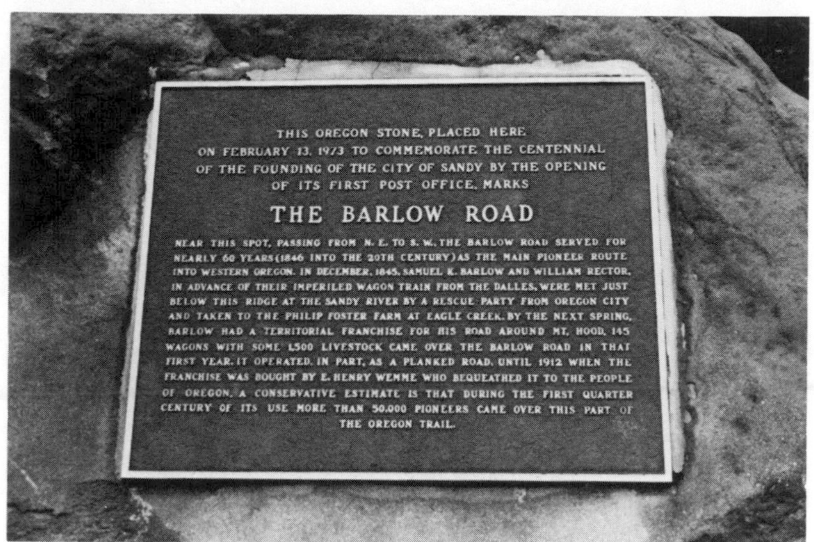

Closeup of bronze plaque on stone monument at Sandy, Oregon, which marks route of Barlow Road.
Author photo

al that we have located provide excellent landmarks. Others give mute testimony to the tragedy that accompanied the pioneer travelers of this trail.

The Barlow Road goes south out of The Dalles and crosses the three mile, five mile, eight mile and 15 mile creeks in succession into Dufur, where Route 197 passes alongside. It then heads for Kingsley and winds along the Tygh Ridge route into the Tygh Valley. Heading southwest out of Tygh Valley the road rises out of a valley that is dotted with an occasional juniper tree. Then the road goes up a steep hill to the Wamic Plateau, with a marker in Wamic. From here to Barlow Pass the trail is primitive. It continues west across three mile Creek Crossing, Rock Creek Crossing and Gate Creek Crossing. Next comes Immigrant Springs, Boulder Creek Crossing, Cedar Creek Crossing and Deep Creek Crossing. White River Hill, Old White River Station, Klinger's Camp and Devil's Half Acre respectively are found every few miles up to Barlow Pass Summit where a U.S. Forest Service marker is located. This is immediately south of Mount Hood.

Heading downhill the trail is brushed out from thick timber growth to the Unknown Pioneer Woman's Grave marker. Here the Barlow Road is quite close to the intersection of Highways 35 and 26. The road proceeds into Summit Meadows, a welcome resting place for pioneer travelers and their livestock.

New bronze plaque being readied for installation at Kelly Field stone marker in Oregon City, Oregon, denoting end of the Barlow Road over the Cascade Mountains and the end of the Oregon Trail.

Author photo

At Government Camp, which is at the entrance to Mount Hood's Timberline Lodge, there is a marker. Here the Barlow Road is on the north side of Highway 26. Beyond is Laurel Hill, the most difficult part of the road, where the steep descent required rope snubbings around trees and log drags to control downhill danger to wagons and oxen. Some stumps today still show these grooves made by repeated rope snubbings.

Once past Laurel Hill, the road crosses the Zigzag River to No. 5 Toll Gate, where there are markers. At Rhododendron is another marker and the Henry Creek Crossing. Shortly, you can see the site of the Hudson Bay Trading Post and Sandy River Crossing. Rock Corral Camp Site has a huge rock that served as a natural fireplace for an overnight stopping place.

The road is on a north ridge above the Sandy River at Marmot. Then past Sievers' Place over the Devil's Backbone for seven miles to Francis Revenue's Place Toll Gate, at the second crossing of the Sandy River. The marker here is alongside of a large black walnut tree planted by Francis Revenue. Both are on private property, so the permission of the present owner should be requested.

In downtown Sandy another marker is located in front of the city hall. Going southwest out of Sandy the road crosses Deep Creek. Original ruts of the road can be seen going downhill into Foster's Place. In Eagle Creek there is a marker on S.E. Eagle Creek Road.

It was necessary to cross the Clackamas River at Feldenheimer's Ford. The road passes Upper Logan and near the Baker Cabin, where there is a marker. Ruts are visible at the south-side yard of Holcomb School. Then the road goes past Holcomb Hill to Abernethy Creek, where there is a new marker at Abernethy Green (Kelly Field) in Oregon City. This new marker denotes the Oregon Trail's end. Another marker, which commemorates the Barlow Road Wagon Train Migration, is in the front yard of the Oregon City courthouse.

From The Dalles to about 15 miles beyond Wamic, the Barlow Road is on private land for a total distance of about 45 miles. For the next 35 miles over Barlow Pass to Zigzag the road is on both private land and in the Mount Hood National Forest. For the remaining 30 miles the road again is on private lands. Most of the markers are readily visible for inspection and photographing.

The route of the Barlow Road Trail is now well established and portions are readily recognizable today. Because much of it is on private land you will have to use the existing roads of the original trail to catch its windings and travels. Thus a series of explorations are in store for the hiker who seeks the challenge of hiking portions of the final leg of the historic Oregon Trail (assuming that permission has been obtained from property owners).

For access to the higher elevation regions of the Barlow Road, you should contact the U.S. Forest Service, Mount Hood National Forest, in Dufur, Bear Springs or Zigzag, regarding road conditions.

East of The Dalles are portions of the original overland Oregon Trail bordering Interstate Highway 80 N from Ontario, Baker, La Grande and Pendleton to The Dalles. The Oregon State Parks and Recreation Branch has established 11 new exhibits along this trail. These interpretative displays, with attractive free standing architecture, are located at rest areas and state parks. Displayed are drawings, maps, photographs and quotations from diaries that depict the story of pioneer covered wagon trains. Information is also available at these exhibits for those who want to hike the nearby remaining and visible portions of the Oregon Trail.

TILLAMOOK HEAD TRAIL - relive the Lewis & Clark Expedition to a coastal view.

One way: six miles; allow three hours one way.
High point: 1200 feet.
Elevation gain: 1100 feet.
Easy one day trip.
Open all year around unless posted.

Tillamook Head

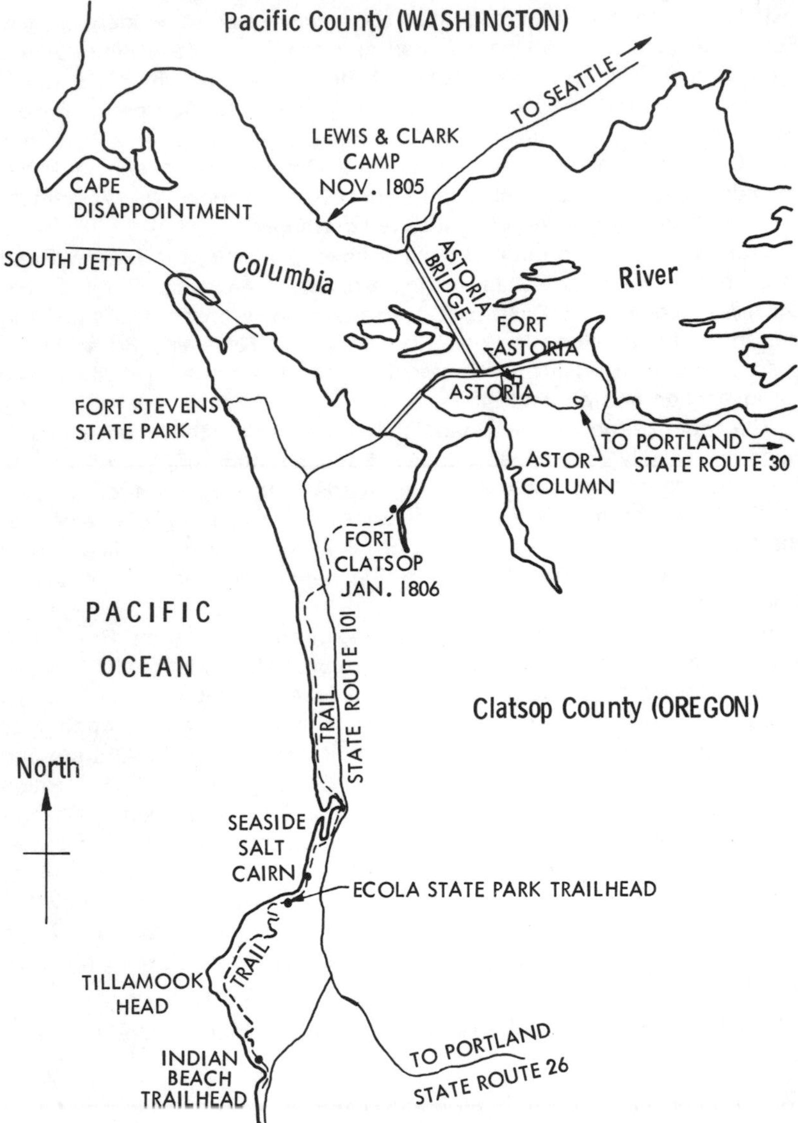

The Lewis and Clark expedition to the Pacific Northwest greatly contributed to our country's development. In tracing some of their footsteps, you can begin to understand regional history.

On January 6, 1806, Clark and a party of 12 set out from their winter quarters at Fort Clatsop to visit the advance team traveling to their salt manufacturing cairn, which today can be seen at Seaside, Oregon. Here they hired an Indian guide to help them reach the south to obtain food from a beached whale. To get there they had to climb Tillamook Head, and as Clark recorded, an ". . . emence mountain the top of which was obscured by the clouds." The following day, in better weather, Clark wrote of the vista," . . . the grandest and most pleasing prospects which my eyes ever surveyed, in my front a boundless ocean . . . the coast as . . . far as my sight could be extended, the Seas raging with emence waves braking with great force."

The original trail up over Tillamook Head was used by the Indians since there was no beach trail available for several miles. A low inland trail around this rocky prominence might have been twice as long. Thus this direct trail goes up to an elevation of 1200 feet and then descends. It was an important coastline route of the Indians.

The six-mile hike is now included in the 62-mile Oregon Coast Trail extending from the Columbia River south jetty to Tillamook Bay. The completed trail is planned to cover the entire Oregon coast. This Tillamook Head crossing is the historical highlight of the coast trail.

Tillamook Rock with abandoned lighthouse at upper left as seen offshore from trail viewing spot on precipitous cliff north of Indian Beach.

Author photo

Looking south, the trail winds down through spruce trees upon approaching the southern end at Indian Beach.

Author photo

The north end of this hike begins at the Ecola State Park boundary trailhead about two miles south of Seaside. The trail begins in thick growth. At about one-half mile, you will encounter a series of switchbacks to a viewpoint. Here, to the north, Seaside and its unobstructed stretch of beach can be seen. The trail continues in the forest for about one and one-half miles at about a 1000 foot elevation.

Soon, at this elevation, you will approach an open area with knee-high grass and a 360 degree view. Here at three and one-half miles from Seaside is a wood marker post on the ocean side. Immediately to the right, in about 30 feet, is the commemorative plaque and a rest bench denoting the spot where Clark enjoyed the beauty of the broad Pacific. You can see the Pacific Ocean and its coastline in a full 360 degree sweep. The view extends past the broad beaches of Seaside and Gearhart to the Coast Mountains at the mouth of the Columbia River, 25 miles north, and as far in the opposite direction to the south.

I have yet to find as commanding a view in all my travels along the Pacific Ocean. Thus in Clark's quest for food, he and his party discovered an outstanding vista that few people have ever experienced. Again, only the hiker can enjoy a thrill such as standing where Clark saw the great Pacific in 1806.

From here, going south, the trail enters a dense forest full of many huge trees that apparently were toppled over by some disastrous Pacific Ocean windstorm. Here switchbacks again can be encountered. Four miles from Seaside is another wood marker at a road crossing. To the right is the Tillamook Hikers Campground. The trail continues inland through a heavy forest partially logged off. Here the needle strewn trail is protected from ocean winds although the forest is open without underbrush.

At about five and one-half miles are good views of the ocean and of Tillamook Rock, with its abandoned lighthouse that is about one mile offshore. These views are dangerously close to vertical coastal cliffs, so be careful. The final portion of the trail runs down through enormous wind swept spruce trees some five feet deep. Indian Beach is in view. Once across the trail, a right turn brings you into the Indian Beach picnic site and parking lot.

Many parts of this trail are wet and muddy even in dry periods. The trail's character constantly changes as it winds from dense forest to open view. It has steady grades thanks to early game and Indian trails. Its well-worn surface indicates that it has been used for a considerable time.

The trail's plant life included sword fern, deer fern, salad and salmonberry. We saw rabbits, chickadees, robins and a hawk. Deer tracks also were visible.

Tillamook Head is a coastal mountain graced by precipitous bluffs, heavy and massive coastal forest growth, little underbrush and soaring gulls. What impressed us was the beauty of this trail, the spaciousness

Lower part of trail consists of switchbacks through thimbleberry brush.

Author photo

of commanding vistas and roar of the powerful surf. It was a memorable experience. Bring a camera, binoculars and water.

To get here from Portland, drive northwest on State Route 26 for 76 miles and join northbound Highway 101 into Seaside. At the southern edge of town turn left (west), cross over the Necanicum River, past the golf course, and again turn left (south) on South Edgemont Road. Drive south about one mile on a gradually rising road to the Ecola State Park parking lot and trailhead sign.

WILLIAM L. FINLEY NATIONAL WILDLIFE REFUGE - a fascinating conservation refuge.

One way: one to seven miles; allow one day.
Pasturelike, agrarian trail.
Easy, leisurely day hike.
Open January through October.

In western-central Oregon south of Corvallis is the William L. Finley National Wildlife Refuge, a chance for an individual hiker or family group to see and experience first-hand a federal conservation resource. Nestled against the eastern foothills of the Coast Range in the broad, Willamette Valley with snow-capped peaks of the Cascades to the east, this refuge of more than 5300 acres is situated on a bird flyway for numerous wintering waterfowl.

William L. Finley Refuge

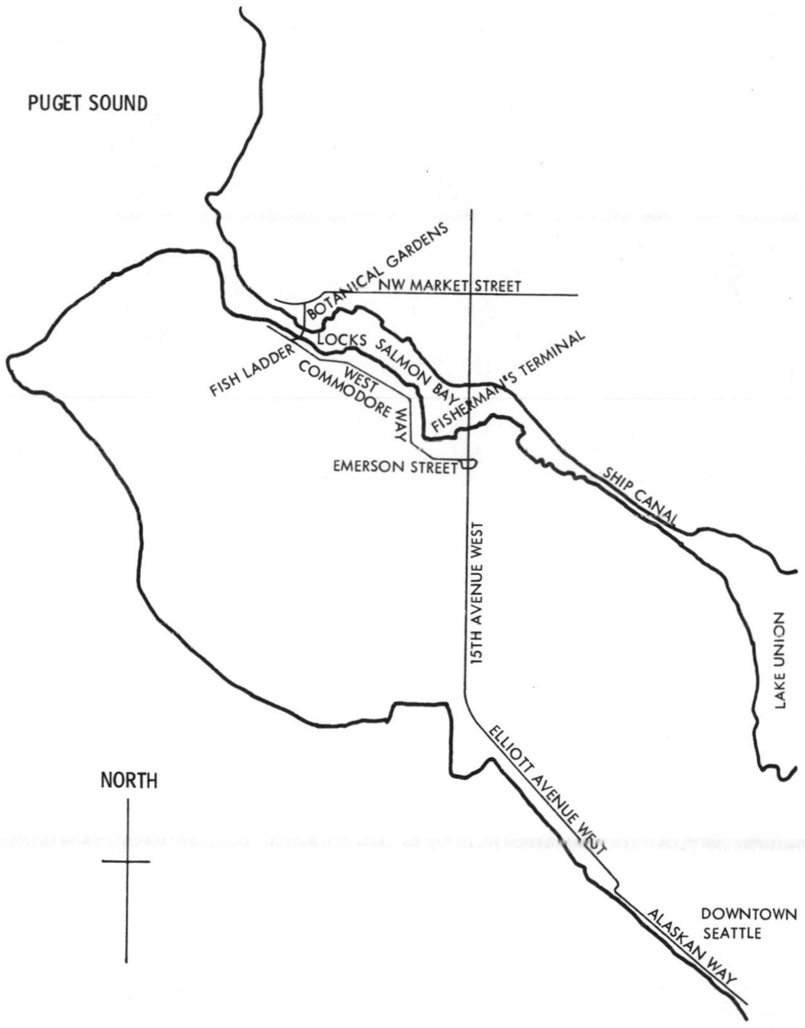

Refuge entrance sign looms prominently on Highway 99W about ten miles south of Corvallis, Oregon.

Author photo

Travelers of the Oregon Trail in the 1840s were the first to settle on the lands that now are within the refuge boundaries. This broad valley with its mild, rainy winter climate is an ideal location for these wintering waterfowl.

Of special interest is the story of a recently threatened species — the dusky Canada goose. This medium-sized, dark brown goose nests entirely in a restricted area along the southeastern coast of Alaska, primarily on the Copper River Delta. Except for stragglers, its whole population winters in the Willamette Valley and along the lower Columbia River. When the future of this small flock of no more than 25,000 seemed questionable, the Department of the Interior's Fish and Wildlife Service decided that protection was needed. Thus three refuges were established at traditional dusky Canada geese concentration points: Ankany, Baskett Slough and with Finley, which is the largest.

Other migratory and resident animals use the same refuge lands. Several species of ducks visit the refuge during migration; wood ducks and hooded mergansers are common summer residents. Blue and ruffed grouse, ring-neck pheasants and California and mountain quail

Bird's nest in tree trunk is found by visitor on one of the many trails at the William L. Finley National Wildlife Refuge in northwest Oregon.

Author photo

are present in varying numbers. The Columbian blacktail deer is common, as are many species of small birds and mammals. In all, 429 species of plants, 193 species of birds, 52 species of mammals and 37 species of fish, amphibians and reptiles have been recorded here.

A system of numerous trails has been established, in addition to ponds and dikes. Extensive fields of such food crops as corn, millet, sudan grass, milo and ryegrass now are grown on the grounds to provide needed winter feed for wildlife. The refuge also serves as an outdoor laboratory for many departments of Oregon State University, which is located only 12 miles north. Bird, mammal and plant lists are available at the refuge headquarters. Hiking, birding, photography and nature observation activities are encouraged here. A birder could spend several days and not cover the possibilities.

There is a large number of individual primitive trails. They wind through a wide variety of habitats — Oregon oak and maple woodlands, Oregon ash thickets, second-growth Douglas fir, brushy hedgerows, marshes, meandering creeks, open meadows, pastures and cultivated fields. In addition ponds, knolls, buttes, prairies, swamps and a few access roads make for a continually changing scene. Day hikes of one to seven miles provide opportunitites to see extensive wildlife. On one of our trips we saw deer, ground squirrels, pheasants, hawks and

Wildlife Ranger shows mounted Dusky Canada Goose specimen to young visitors on day hike at the William L. Finley National Wildlife Refuge. This species of Canadian goose migrates from Alaska to winter in Oregon's Willamette River Valley area.
Author photo

a golden eagle yet to which we had the entire area to ourselves.

There are special viewing locations and informative outdoor displays. The main attraction of this fine preserve is the variety of things to see in their native rural settings.

The refuge is available for day visits only. The nearest campgrounds are at Alsea Falls or Corvallis.

To get to Finley refuge from Portland, Oregon, drive 69 miles south on Interstate 5 to Albany. Go five miles past Albany to junction of State Route 34. Turn right, or west, for nine miles to Corvallis. Turn left, or south, onto Highway 99W. Go south for 10 miles, where you are greeted with a large entrance sign on the right. Turn right and follow the road for about 2 and one-half miles to a parking area by the refuge office and large red barn.

6 Washington

The Evergreen State is well named since its mild climate, with its even rainfall, keeps the foliage green in most of the western portion of the state throughout the year. From the hiker's standpoint, this half of the state — a region perhaps 200 miles wide and 240 miles long, with its mountain ranges, dense forests, beautiful lakes and hundreds of miles of Pacific Ocean coastline—is a veritable hiking heaven. When the western slopes are overcast with rain, the hiker can head for the sunny eastern slopes of the Cascades. Most of the eastern half of the state is dry plateau land, and much of it is irrigated to produce fruit and agricultural crops.

It is believed that the earliest explorations of this region were made by the Spanish, who operated out of Mexico 400 years ago. There is the possible exception of Orientals who may have sailed or drifted to Washington shores. In 1792 Captain George Vancouver explored the inland water of what is now Washington State and he gave British names to most of the prominent snowcapped peaks. He thus honored his superiors in the Royal Navy (Rainier and Hood) and his officer (Baker).

The French Canadian fur traders probably were the first white men to utilize the game trails that the Indians had used, although both groups used the rivers and streams wherever possible. The dense foothill underbrush and the Puget Sound country were deterrents to easy cross-state traffic, and cascades were a formidable barrier. Most of the settlers of the Puget Sound country came by ship and not by covered wagon. However, there were settlers that turned north at The Dalles to follow the Naches River across Naches Pass to the Greenwater River and Puget Sound.

By the 1800s the Washington Indian-trail network included seven east-west trails from the Columbia to the Skagit and Stehekin Rivers. The main north-south trail extended from what is now Portland to Olympia, Seattle and Bellingham. Another trail began east of the Cascades in Columbia City and extended to Yakima, Ellensburg, Wenatchee and Chelan.

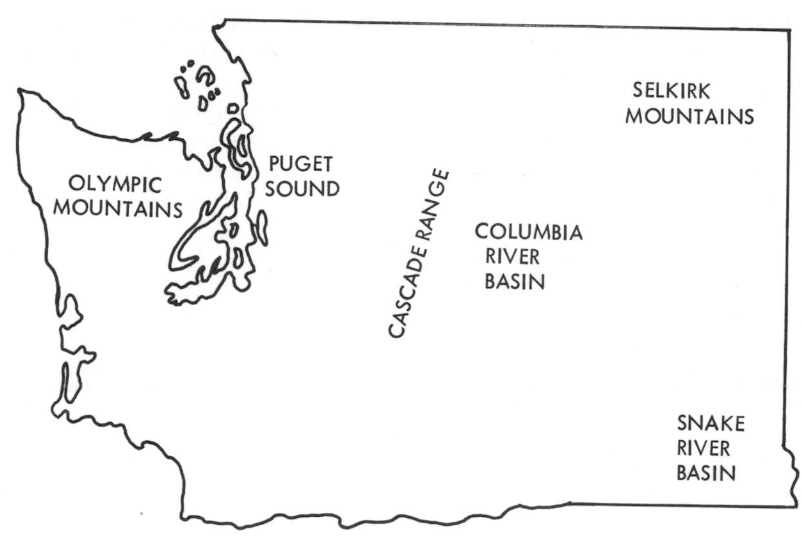

WASHINGTON

Washington, like Oregon, has several mountain ranges running north and south — the Olympics, the Cascades and Selkirks. These separate the coast, Puget Sound and the coulee reclamation country. Each of the six regions has unique hiking challenges. Washington provides the lure of seven snowcapped peaks, each standing above 9000 feet, that attrack hiking and climbing enthusiasts. They are Rainier, Baker, St. Helens, Adams, Shuksan, Glacier and Stuart. Each has a recreational area.

The hiking regions are well known and well documented. In successive order, starting at the coast and moving east, are the Olympic National Park coast strip, the Olympic Mountains with its rain forests, the Puget Sound lowland trails, the North Cascades, the Central Cascades including Mount Rainier and the Southern Cascades with Mount St. Helens and Adams. East of the Cascades are the Okanogan and Colville National forests.

It is estimated that Washington's population of over three and one-half million has generated some 300,000 hikers and climbers, possibly 200,000 in the Puget Sound region alone. There is concern that there maybe an over use of hiking and camping facilities. Reservations are required for overnight hikers in some of the areas.

About one fourth of the state's land is set aside for national parks, forests and recreation areas. Regarding national parks size, the Olympic National Park is the largest. Next is the North Cascades National Park located at the state's northern boundary. Mount Rainier is the oldest and best developed.

The national forests cover most of the Cascade Range, surround the Olympic Mountains and touch the northeast and southeast corners of the state. The nine national forests are: Olympic, Mount Baker, Okanogan, Wenatchee, Snoqualmie, Gifford Pinchot, Colville, Kaniksu and Umatilla.

Three national recreation areas are Coulee Dam, Lake Chelan and Ross Lake. Two wilderness areas have been established at Glacier Peak and Pasayten.

In addition there are 140 developed state parks. Hiking trails are included in about 20 of these. There also are about 30 undeveloped recreation areas, many of which are planned to feature hiking opportunities.

Privately operated recreation areas, which can be enjoyed by the public, are made available by ten lumber and power companies. To obtain the list, write to the Washington State Parks and Recreation Commission in Olympia.

The Stevens-Van Trump monument is a stone memorial in the form of a bench seat providing a rest stop for hikers.

Robert E. Oestreich photo

The Stevens-Van Trump monument as seen from the rear faces Mt. Rainier above Paradise Park.
Robert E. Oestreich photo

Weathered stump on Hurricane Ridge in Olympic National Park in Washington.

Barbara Newell photo

Outlet to Spectacle Lake in Kittitas County, Washington.

Dick Bolding photo

Spectacle Lake in Kittitas County, Washington, as seen from the ridge to the south.
Dick Bolding photo

Glacier Lake in Kittitas County, Washington
Dick Bolding photo

Upper Puyallup River in Pierce County, Washington.

Dick Bolding photo

Black tail fawn seen in western Washington.
Dick Bolding photo

Basin between Chikamin and Lyman Peak in Kittitas County, Washington.

Dick Bolding photo

Backpacking hikers on Pacific Ocean trail of Olympic National Park strip provide action profiles against ocean surf during blustery winter day.
Keith Gunnar photo

Chikamin Peak and lake in Kittitas County, Washington.

Dick Bolding photo

Mount Rainier as seen from Pinnacle Park trail. Magnificent vistas can be the rewards for hikers who venture into the high country.
Robert E. Oestreich photo

Many Washington hikers constantly return to their favorite hiking areas. Some have a deep love for Mount Rainier or the Olympic Mountains. For example, consider the appeal of The Wonderland Trail around Mount Rainier. The 90-mile trail crosses snowfields, skirts glaciers and winds through forests, meadows and alpine lakes. The trail has a layout that can be hiked in segments or in 10 continuous days. Dozens of other trails tie into The Wonderland Trail.

Other hikers like to do a specific area once each year. A popular area is the Enchanted Lakes trail south of Leavenworth. Some regularly haunt the Pacific Ocean beaches to see the changes brought about by tides and winds and to beachcomb oddities at the high tide line. Within the Olympic National Park is the 20-mile LaPush-Ozette beach hike, an all-season favorite for many hiking groups.

The Washington portion of the Pacific Crest Trail is thought to be the most scenic. It begins at the Columbia River near Cascade Locks and follows the crest of the Cascades to White Pass, Chinook Pass, Naches Pass, Snoqualmie Pass, Stevens Pass and Harts Pass. Only those who have organized food and gear deliveries will attempt this 475-mile trek.

Other more popular areas are the North Cascades National Park, Okanogan National Forest, Wenatchee National Forest, Mount Baker National Forest, Snoqualmie National Forest, Glacier Peak Wilderness and the Olympic National Park.

Vacation day hikes or weekend overnights are planned well in advance, rain or shine. Many newcomers join hiking clubs, others charge ahead with their *101 Hikes in the North Cascades* in hand. Again, not all hikers are backpackers. For some a complete hiking outfit consists of hiking boots, a rucksack, Levi's, shirt and a copy of *Footloose around Puget Sound.*

The grandeur of snow-covered Mount Rainier, Baker, Adams and St. Helens, all part of the Cascades yet rising abruptly from the surrounding terrain, is characteristic of Washington hiking. The entire Olympic Range is yet another exciting story. There is a bevy of hiking trails to cover, all with challenges, from seashore to alpine levels. Because of the great number of hiking trails, a mild climate and the enthusiasm of its residents to pursue outdoor recreation, Washington leads other states of the Pacific Northwest in hiking opportunities.

PACIFIC NORTHWEST NATIONAL SCENIC TRAIL

Legislation is now pending before Congress to establish a Pacific Northwest trail that would extend from the Rocky Mountains in Montana to the Olympic Mountains in Washington. The bill recommends that the Pacific Northwest National Scenic Trail be added to the list of study trails under the National Trails System Act of 1968. Most of the trail would parallel the U.S. - Canadian border and begin at Glacier National Park through Idaho and Eastern Washington, over the Cascades Mountains and culminate in crossing the Olympics to the Pacific Ocean.

The trail would bring hikers to some of the most spectacular scenery in the country. The creation of the Pacific Northwest trail would be a worthy addition to our national hiking path network, which includes the Appalachian Trail and the Cascade Crest Trail.

This proposal is before the Interior and Insular Affairs Subcommittee on National Parks and Recreation.

This proposed 700-mile trail closely follows the 49th parallel except for its last part—through the Puget Sound country where generally it stays above the 48th parallel. It would cross the Lewis Range, the Continental Divide, the Purcell Mountains, the Cabinet Mountains of the Bitterroot Range and the Okanogan Highlands. It would go north of the North Cascades National Park, around Mt. Baker, down the Skagit Riv-

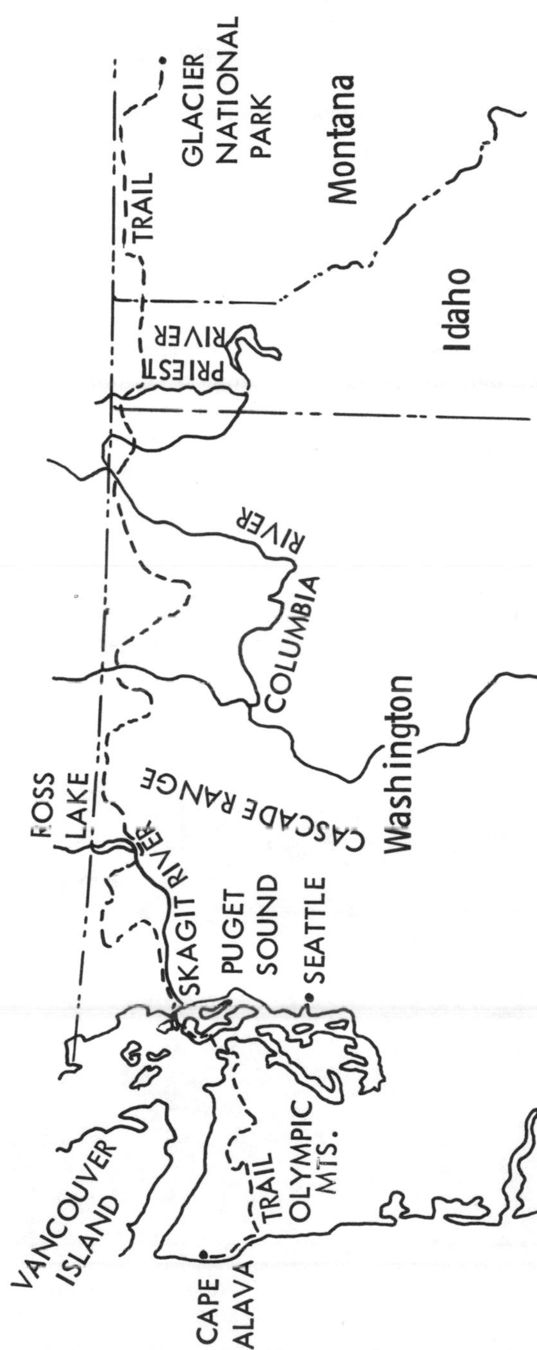

Proposed Pacific Northwest National Scenic Trail

er to Whidbey Island, through the Olympic Mountains to the Pacific Ocean coast and finally north to the archeological dig at Cape Alava.

BURKE-GILMAN TRAIL - A multi-use urban trail.

One way: 12 miles; allow full day.
High Point: 100 feet.
Low Point: 40 feet.
Surface trail for hikers, joggers and bicyclists.
Open year-round.

With no exceptions, the busiest hiking path in the entire Pacific Northwest is a recently established trail on an abandoned Burlington Northern railroad bed in Seattle, Washington. Extending east and west across the mid-point of the city, the trail starts at Discovery Park, which overlooks Puget Sound, and proceeds east—past Lake Union, the University of Washington and Sand Point—to Kenmore on Lake Washington. Never has such a project been the focus of so much public response, both pro and con. Environmentalists fought for the trail while border residents fought against it. The city arranged a land trade with the railroad, and now the trail is being developed in segments.

The trail is named for two pioneers, Seattle civic leaders, who led the movement in the 1880s to build the old Seattle, Lake Shore and Eastern Railroad, which would link Seattle with a Canadian transcontinental line. The trial is being developed by the city, the University of Washington and the county.

Trail follows old railroad bed heading towards the University of Washington from the west.
Author photo

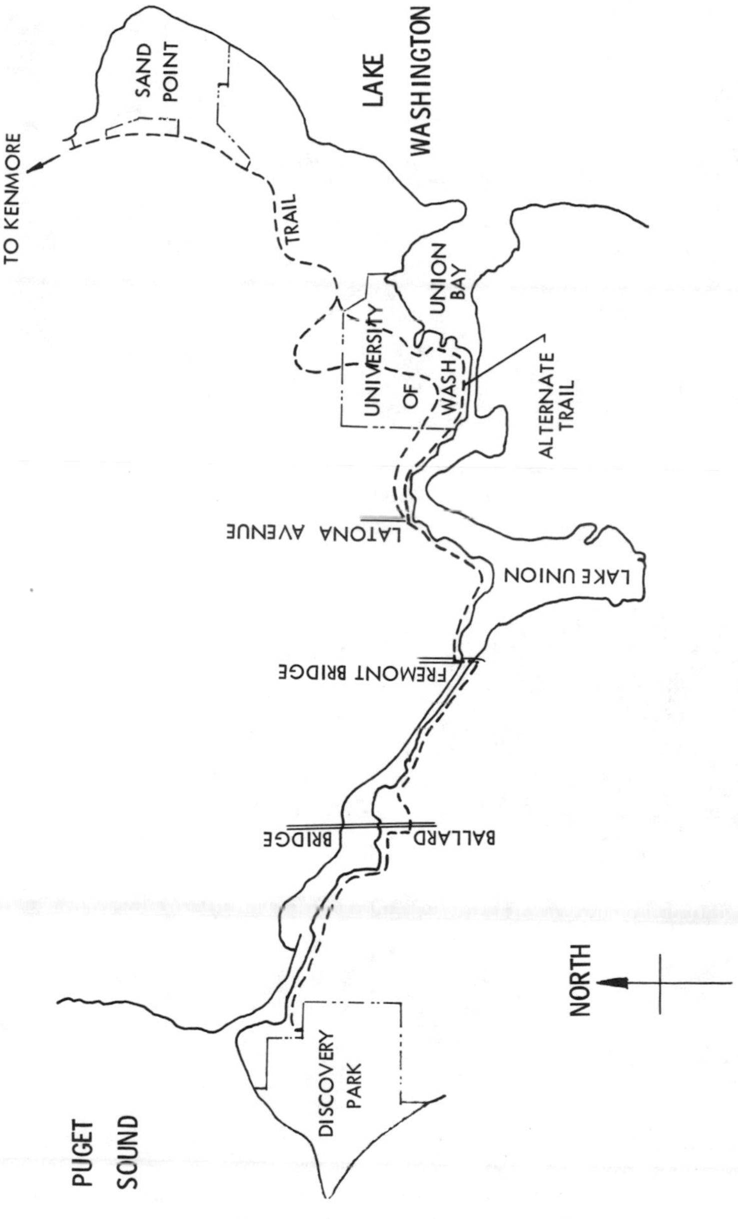

Burke-Gilman
TO KENMORE
SAND POINT
LAKE WASHINGTON
TRAIL
UNION BAY
UNIVERSITY OF WASH
ALTERNATE TRAIL
LATONA AVENUE
LAKE UNION
FREMONT BRIDGE
BALLARD BRIDGE
NORTH
DISCOVERY PARK
PUGET SOUND

Alternate route of Burke-Gilman trail through the University of Washington along ship canal and under Montlake bridge.

Author photo

Alternate route of hiking path through University of Washington west of canoe house.

Author photo

Hiking trail uses former railroad trestle to cross busy city street.

Author photo

One developed segment has a bituminous-paved trail that is 12 feet wide, which accommodates hikers and bikers. A four-foot wide gravel trail that runs alongside has been included for joggers. Motor vehicles and horses are prohibited. Buffering the trail from adjacent properties, the inclusion of safety lighting, signs, litter cans, rest and view areas, landscaping and installation of street crossing signs have been accomplished. The trail utilizes former railroad trestles. Elsewhere it moves under pedestrian walkways.

You can see retired couples picking blackberries that grow along the side, youthful bicyclists going their way, joggers stepping along, determined hikers seeking a distant objective, family groups ambling along and students chatting as they walk with abandon. This limited-access multi-purpose trail is used by thousands of people. It is estimated that 2000 daily bicycle commuters are using different portions of the trail.

The trail winds along in places that are completely hidden only to emerge, in a short distance, onto an overpass above a busy street. It curves behind homes, commercial buildings and clinics, through the greenery of the university campus and along the ship canal. It is a long, park-like trail that always changes—full of happy strangers who greet each other. A camaraderie exists here as a national park's alpine trail. Here people wear packs, but there are lots of rucksacks.

To travel the entire trail, start at Discovery Park. Take West Commodore Way east past the locks along the Salmon Bay Waterway and Terminal. Cross Nickerson Street to Ewing Mini Park. Follow east to the Fremont bridge, and go across to the north side of Lake Union past the Gas Works Park. Continue on Northlake Way to Latona Avenue (where you can join the beginning of the railroad route or take an alternate route along the water's edge under the Montlake bridge past the university canoe house and stadium to pick up the railroad bed level trail again at N.E. 47th junction). From here follow the railroad route east to Sand Point, Matthews Beach and Kenmore.

To get to Discovery Park from downtown Seattle, take Alaskan Way and Elliot Avenue along the waterfront to Smith Cove, and take the Magnolia bridge to the Magnolia district. Go north on 34th Avenue West to West Emerson Street and turn left. On 40th Avenue West turn right again, or north, to the Discovery Park entrance. There also are bus connections that leave from Seattle and go to Discovery Park (take Fort Lawton bus) and Kenmore (take Bothel bus).

CARBON RIVER GLACIER - a trail to one of Mount Rainier's many glaciers.

One way: Three and one-half miles; allow one and one-half hours one way.
High point: 4000 feet.
Elevation gain: 1700 feet.
Easy trail along Carbon River bed.
Best time: July through September.

One of the advantages of hiking the Pacific Northwest is the existence of glacier fields. From where we eat breakfast in our Mercer Island home, we can see Mount Rainier with its massive glacier system to the southeast—exactly 53 miles away. From the mountain's summit, in direct line of our sight, is the Carbon River Glacier, which slowly creeps down the mountain side.

Carbon River glacier extends the farthest distance away from the summit of all Mount Rainier's 22 glaciers. Since the edge of the glacier is only 46 miles, air line, from our home, we picked it for our glacier hike. There are many beautiful glacier vistas on Mount Rainier, and most are quite photogenic. There are numerous other glacier fields in Washington, both in the Cascade and Olympic Ranges. If you visit any

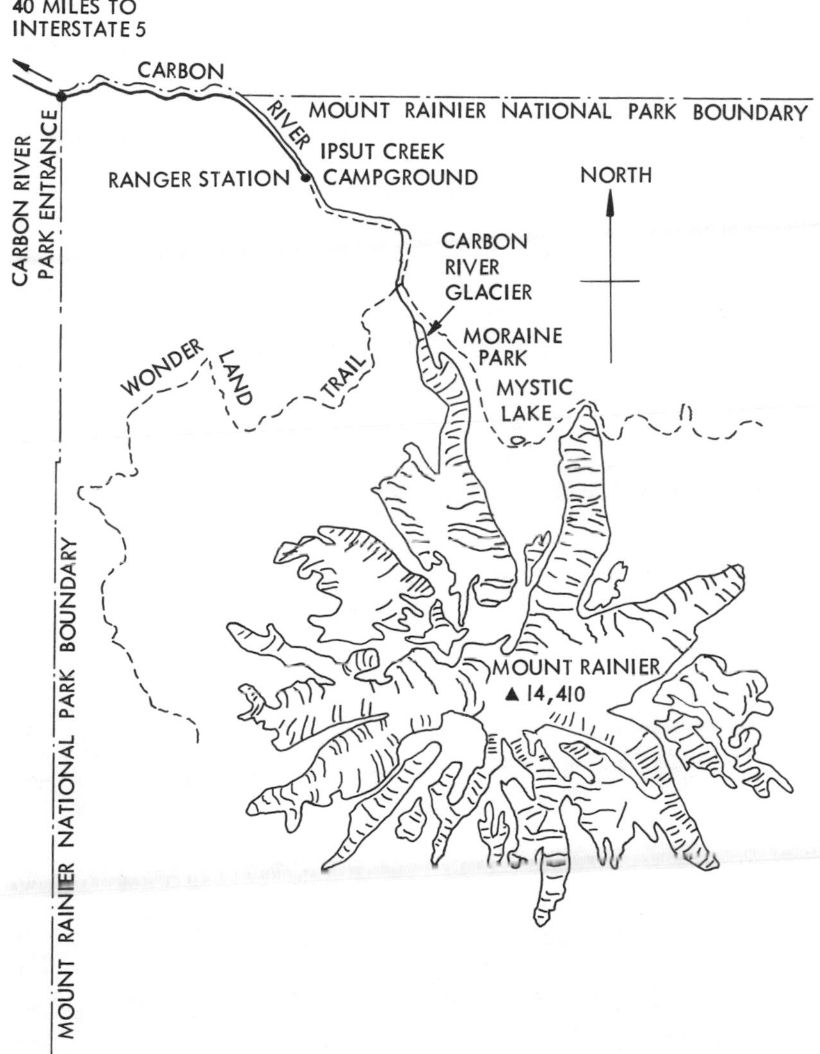

Carbon River Glacier

one of these, you will begin to crave more.

The Carbon River Glacier is three and one-half miles in from the Ipsut Creek Campground at the extreme northwest corner of Mount Rainier National Park. From the trailhead the first one-half mile is on a wide, easy trail of even grade. For the next mile, it continues to follow the forested valley floor close to the river elevation.

At the first trail junction, follow marker directions to the left across the Carbon River. Glacier moraine all across the wide river bed, the milky colored condition of the water and a blast of icy cold air force us to continue upstream. Here at the river bed the summit of Mount Rainier can be seen eight miles away.

On the east side of the Carbon River, the trail heads south and steepens with switchbacks. Huge windfalls crisscross the river bed. At the next trail junction keep to the right. For the next mile the needle laden trail leads through a quiet, primitive forest where trees have moss-covered exposed roots, and slippery log footbridges, across streams, have helpful side handrails. Soon you will find the junction with the Wonderland Trail, which circuits the entire glacier system of Mount Rainier. At this point the trees begin to thin out.

Continuing up the valley, you will soon see the glacier. In another one-half mile, on a rock ledge trail, the glacier snout is quite dirty and unattractive and difficult to photograph—unlike the glacier's beginning in its upper reaches. This glacier is well named since it has a layer of dirt and rock on its upper exposed surface. Even the ice is dirty where it sloughs off in huge chunks. Small streams emerge from under the

At the Carbon River trail crossing about a mile downstream from the glacier this wide moraine rock bed testifies to former torrential river flows.
Author photo

Suspension foot bridge across Carbon River used by hikers heading west on the wonderland trail.
Author photo

trail's unsightly ice face, which gives birth to the Carbon River. A sign warns hikers not to approach the face of the glacier because of possible danger from breaking ice and boulders, which roll down from the top. You only have to sit still for a few minutes alongside the trail to see these very things happen.

Other glacier views are to be seen farther up the trail. In another two miles, you can reach Moraine Park, and an additional mile up to Mystic Lake takes you to an elevation of 6000 feet after a steep ascent, a gain of 3700 feet from the trailhead.

We saw lots of deer fern, ocean spray and alpine fir. This area is reported to be one of the wettest in the state with an annual rainfall of 100 inches, thus the woodland appearance here is similar to the Olympic Rain Forest. About a mile down the glacier on the east side of the trail is a good size tree blaze, one worth watching for.

We did this hike once in mid-February during a year without snow. We did not see a single person on the trail. We did see a few footprints that appeared to be about a week old. We stopped at the river crossing on our return for a drink of glacier stream, which tasted even better than the well water at home. We saw several washed-out, dry river beds that had previously contained raging torrents.

We saw humming birds, chickadees and chipmunks—but deer tracks only. Several birds flew nearby but were quiet and not recognizable in the dense dark forest region.

To get to the Carbon Glacier from Seattle, drive south on Interstate 5 towards Tacoma. At about 23 miles, take Mount Rainier Exit 142B and go west for about one-quarter mile to the stoplight. Turn left (south) onto State Route 161S towards Puyallup. In about seven miles,

The snout of the Carbon River Glacier is shown slowly grinding and squeezing its way through the rock-walled valley.

Author photo

after crossing the Puyallup River, turn left (east) onto State Route 410E towards Yakima. Do not go into the city of Puyallup as the Mount Rainier signs might indicate, for these signs now lead to a different Mount Rainier entrance. When on route 410E, you will see Mount Rainier directly ahead. (In the springtime this broad flat valley near Puyallup is covered with fields of daffodils and tulips.)

Follow 410E for 14 miles towards Buckley. Watch for logging truck activity on weekdays. When you reach the intersection with State Route 162, turn right (south) for two miles and then bear left on State Route 165 towards Wilkeson. Watch for a bridge with one-way traffic. Past Carbonado the narrow road hugs the deep gorge of the Carbon River. In a short time, take a left at the Carbon River Entrance sign. The road is gravel for a distance and is then paved. Soon you will see the beautiful river valley. The park entrance is 22 miles from Buckley. Another five miles will bring you inside the park boundary, and an easily graded gravel road brings you to the Ranger Station. Here you should check in and get a set of park rules. The Ipsut Creek Campground is a short distance ahead. Park here by the trailhead.

For this hike, the best weather gauge is if you can see Mount Rainier from Seattle and there is no cap cloud around its peak. It is possible to do this hike in an afternoon, but with a morning start there are more options for side trips. When the weather is overcast, expect rain at the trail elevations.

What did we especially remember about this hike? First, we were vulnerable to Mount Rainier's majesty. Second, we experienced a pleasant soft feeling in our hiking boots from the needle strewn trail. Third, we remember the wind protection of the deep, forested trail. Finally, we loved the easy, steady downhill return.

DOSEWALLIPS-ELWHA TRAIL - visit Olympic Mountain alpine meadows area.

One way: 42 miles; allow four to five days.
High point: 5847 feet.
Elevation gain: 3847 feet.
Backpack trip for experienced hikers.
Open July through September.

This hike is included because it is representative of the many beautiful trails in the Olympic Mountains contained within the Olympic National Park located in the northwestern region of Washington state. This trail goes through scenic alpine meadows, and at Hayden Pass provides a breathtaking vista for viewing the high snowcapped peaks of the range. The Dose Meadows here are well known for their many varieties of alpine flowers.

The trail starts from the east border of the Olympic National Park and goes west to the Hayes River Ranger Station located centrally in the park. It then heads north along the Elwha River to meet the trailhead at Whisky Bend. The park has many other cross trails, some entering from the south and west as well as others from the north. Around its perimeter there are over 20 accesses into the park's 600 miles of trails.

The hike starts at the Dosewallips Ranger Station. Here is where you register and obtain a backcountry use permit required for all overnight travel. All hikers are urged to abide by the park rules and regulations such as keeping to the established fire rings campfires. Much damage has occurred by hikers setting up their own campsites. The campground near the Ranger Station is roomy and well maintained, a good place for the first overnight. Starting at an elevation of 2000 feet the trail heads along the north bank of the Dosewallips River through thick virgin Douglas fir and western hemlock before breaking out into high country meadows. This first portion of the hike is steeper than the remaining part.

Bear Camp shelter is in 11 miles at 3844 feet. Then comes Dose Meadows shelter at 12.8 miles and Hayden Meadows a short way beyond. The trail from Hayden Meadows to Hayden Pass is often snow covered. Here the grade steepens. Hayden Meadows is filled with wild flowers and streams and is a sight to behold.

Hayden Pass is in 15.4 miles at an elevation of 5847 feet. At and beyond the pass are stupendous panoramic views of Mount Olympus

Dosewallips-Elwha

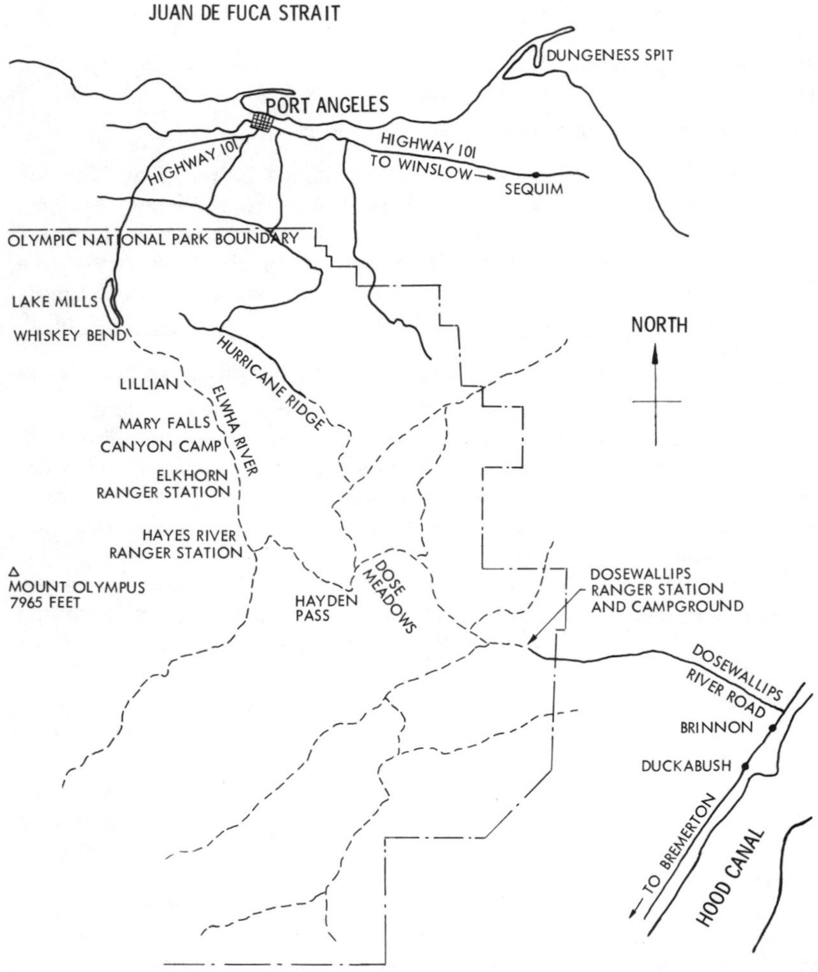

Hayden Pass is popular hiking objective from the northern and eastern sides of the Olympic National Park.

Duane Oyler photo

and other snowcapped peaks of the Olympic Mountains immediately to the west. The trail continues steadily down 9.6 miles to where the Hayes River meets the northbound Elwha River. This is near the Hayes River Ranger Station and is at 1685 feet elevation.

Going north one passes Elkhorn Ranger Station, Canyon Camp, Mary Falls, and Lillian to the trailhead at Whiskey Bend at 1100 feet elevation near the south end of Lake Mills. The road goes north out of the park to join State Route 101 into Port Angeles.

For general weather in the summer months this hike will be in the lee of the higher portions of the Olympic Range and will be dryer than the windward Pacific Ocean side. This may be one of the dryer hikes in the Olympics. This area experiences 50-60 inches of annual rainfall compared to the west side, in the rain forest, which has over twice that amount. We have hiked this trail in August with sun every day and no rain, but then again in July during another year we had plenty of rain—so plan accordingly.

Much can be learned from a short chat with the trail rangers who are most helpful. They are well versed on the flora and fauna. There is plenty of wildlife in the park. Expect to see deer, marmots, raccoon,

Red mountainheath and mountain buckwheat are plant subjects of interest to hiker at Hayden Pass in Olympic National Park.

Duane Oyler photo

Hiker on Hayden Pass trail passes fields of avalanche fawnlilies. Part of trail is seen in upper right.

Duane Oyler photo

skunk, squirrels, an occasional elk and possibly a black bear. The chance of a visit by a bear means a pack and food cache at least 12 feet off the ground.

About 140 species of birds have been identified in the park. One of the highlights of this hike along the Elwha River and its tributaries is to watch for the water ouzle, a bird which will feed under water along the stream bottom then fly out as if all birds do this.

Expect to see lots of timber. The western hemlock, Sitka spruce, western redcedar, bigleaf maple frequent the lower elevations. Farther up look for the Pacific silver fir, western white pine, Douglas fir and western hemlock.

To get to this trailhead from downtown Seattle, take the Bremerton ferry across Puget Sound. This 60 minute crossing to Bremerton on a clear day presents the entire Olympic Mountain skyline spread out in the west. On landing in Bremerton follow State Route 304 one mile west to State Route 3, where you turn left (south). Travel 3.8 miles to Gorst, and another 9 miles to Belfair. One mile beyond Belfair turn right on State Route 106 and follow Hood Canal. About 5 miles past Union join State Route 101 going north, and drive 30 miles to Brinnon. About one mile past Brinnon turn left at Dosewallips River Road sign.

Field of avalanche fawnlilies near Hayden Pass present alpine floral beauty.

Nancy Oyler photo

The road follows the river about 16 miles to trailhead and Dosewallips Ranger Station.

This is a hike where transportation is needed at the north end of the trail. From Whiskey Bend trailhead there is a more direct route back to Seattle. Going north out of the park the road goes to Port Angeles, a good place for an overnight stop if one's schedule permits.

Take State Route 101 east from Port Angeles about 30 miles past Sequim and Discovery Bay. At three miles beyond Discovery Bay bear left onto State Route 104 for 15 miles including crossing the mile and a half long Hood Canal toll floating bridge (concrete pontoons). Turn right at end of the bridge onto State Route 3 for seven miles then left onto State Route 305 for 15 miles past Poulsbo and across the Agate Pass bridge to Winslow. Here the ferry gives you a 30 minute scenic return trip across Puget Sound to Seattle amid a backdrop of the Cascade Mountains to the east. If this run is at night the city lights, across the water will leave a striking impression, one to be long remembered.

Much has been written about hiking the many other trails in the Olympic National Park. The backpacker still has much to explore. If his forte is glaciers there are 60 in all here. In addition day hikes within the park are popular with visitors to Port Angeles. From here it is an interesting drive to the Hurricane Ridge area which affords outstanding vistas and opportunities for rucksack exploring.

EBEY'S LANDING - scenic ocean strait and site of early settler massacre.

One way: four miles; allow three hours.
Dirt paths on bluff and gravel sandy beach.
Interesting half day hike.
Good any season.

On this hike, you will get a sense of Pacific Northwest history that is enhanced by seacoast beauty and ocean trail beachcombing. Ebey's Landing is the location where Colonel Isaac Ebey was massacred in August 1857, during an Indian uprising.

Ebey's Landing

Typical beach scene looking toward Ebey's Landing. Excellent beachcombing is found here due to westward exposure from the Pacific Ocean through the Juan de Fuca Strait.

Author photo

Few hikes can match this for sheer scenic beauty. The trail moves along the top of a sloping salt-water bluff, that faces the Strait of Juan de Fuca from the western-most beach of Whidbey Island, Washington. Past the shipping lanes, Vancouver Island is visible to the right and to the left Port Townsend and, behind, Olympic Mountain can be seen. Ships headed for the Pacific, towing barges and Alaska bound cargo fleets can be seen while you hike this relatively easy trail.

The weather is mild every season. Since central Whidbey Island is sheltered by the Olympic Mountains from the coastal prevailing winds, this region is referred to as Western Washington's "banana belt." Expect dry, cool, windy but clear weather.

En route to the hike, be sure to enjoy some of the neighborhood scenes near Prairie Center. Here, in excellent farming country, are original homesteads. Visit the blockhouses still standing, the quaint cemetery and the monument depicting the site of the Indian massacre. Since most commemorative memorials are built with public money, this one is unique since it was thoughtfully built by a private individual, the late Frank Pratt, Jr.

The trail follows a portion of Whidbey Island's western coastline, which is blessed with good beachcombing. Pacific Ocean currents and winds bring floating debris directly to this beachline through the Strait of Juan de Fuca. Driftwood, fishing gear, agates, shells and bottles of

The Ebey residence and barn where Indian massacre took place in 1857. Other members of the Ebey family and guests escaped being killed by hiding in the brush behind farmhouse.

Author photo

Heading north the trail on the ridge goes through volunteer wheat growing outside fenced wheat field at the right.

Author photo

Marker on bluff depicts where Colonel Isaac Ebey was murdered by Haida Indians. This was done to avenge the death of one of their chiefs killed at Port Gamble.

Author photo

oriental origin can be found here in any season. While hiking the trail and enjoying the natural beauty of the setting, your casual glance westward out from the strait conjures up all sorts of images that are associated with our Japanese neighbors some 5000 miles away.

This is a scenic trail in an isolated and untouched region. The hike, in opposite directions like many done in the Pacific Northwest, can be made with two couples and a car for each heading the trail. To hike the northbound leg, park at Ebey's Landing. About 200 yards north, watch for the trail to veer up the side of the bluff and skirt a cultivated field. The trail then rises to a second 100-foot elevation rise and passes alongside a forest-edge with picturesque, windswept trees. Here is a stupendous view! At about the one-mile point, you will overlook a half mile long log-filled lagoon, several hundred feet below this sloping bank, that is named Perego's Lake for a Civil War veteran who homesteaded here in 1876.

Small cacti, incongruous in relation to this environment, cover the bank above Perego's Lake. If you must go down to the lagoon, be careful. Try not to slide or fall down. The cactus spines break off in short lengths and are not easily removed. On one trip we took this shortcut to the lagoon, but we will not make the same mistake again. Sheep used to graze here, so there are many narrow parallel paths.

Approximately one-half mile farther, the trail diagonals down to the beach.

Continue north along the beach to Partridge Point beach area. Farther on the Partridge Point fog horn can be seen up on the bluff. Directly east of the fog horn lies the abandoned Fort Ebey, which was once strategically important, that will be restored as a state park. A small driftwood filled lagoon can be reached in 200 feet. At the south end of this lagoon is a side trail that leads up to old Fort Ebey. A second side trail from the north end of the lagoon leads to Lake Pondilla, serene and woodsy.

A short distance north, precariously perched on the edge of the beach bluff, remains of World War II concrete coastal fortifications can be seen. Immediately beyond is Libbey Park, an Island County waterfront park and picnic site with adequate parking. Here the southbound couple's car is parked. They arrived after driving past Coupeville to the northwest corner of Penn Cove, turning left from State Route 20 onto Libbey Road, and going west to its termination at Libbey Park.

We saw an occasional deer and island rabbits. Goldfinches, red-wing blackbirds, soaring kingfishers, gulls and an occasional hawk grace this bluff. Wildflowers, in season, carpet the trail.

Ridge senteniel alongside upper trail frames in the distance Colonel Ebey's farmhouse, Ebey's Landing, and multiple drift tide lines on adjoining beach.
Author photo

To get to Ebey's Landing from Seattle, follow the same instructions previously given for Fort Casey on Whidbey Island—namely, Interstate 5 to the Mukilteo Ferry, then drive 26 miles to Coupeville. From State Route 20, turn left on Engle Road to Prairie Center. Here take a right onto Ebey Road. To visit the blockhouse in the cemetery, turn right on Cook Road and go up the hill toward the trees. Another left brings you to the cemetery. Returning to Ebey Road, drive west towards the beach. The Ebey homestead is to the left as you approach the bluff. Before driving down to the beach, stop and visit the memorial marker to the left. Parking is to the right at the beach level.

This is one of our favorite hikes, one that we try to do every year. Elaine and the youngsters love it here. As a youngster, Elaine vacationed here in the summers. This hike has many pleasant memories for us. Carry water, camera and binoculars.

Federated Forest State Park - a pioneer trail.

One way circuit: two miles; allow two hours.
Base elevation: 1700 feet.
Easy half-day walk.
Open all year around.

Although Orientals may have been the first to reach the Pacific Northwest, the earliest known explorers were the Spanish and British who came by ship. Later, fur traders came here from Eastern Canada, sailing the Thompson and Columbia rivers. Mountain crossings were known to be formidable, dangerous and seasonal. As more settlers pushed across the plains of the United States toward the Oregon Territory, certain foot trails became wagon trails.

In Washington the Naches trail, one of the first pioneer trails between the eastern side of the Cascades and the Puget Sound country, passes through the Federation Forest of the Snoqualmie National Forest. Westward migration of settlers necessitated an improvement of the Indian trail between Fort Walla Walla in eastern Washington and Fort Steilacoom in western Washington. In 1853 work was begun, from the west end toward Naches Pass, to widen this trail for wagon travel. At this time the westbound Longmire-Biles wagon train, made up of over 100 people, begun in the eastern side of the Cascades crisscrossing the Naches River toward the pass. On the west side, south of Pyramid Peak, they had to lower their wagons down a steep 1000-foot drop to the west-flowing Greenwater River and the White River. They became the first party to cross the Washington Cascades.

In 1854 this route was used by another wagon train as well as the U.S. Army during Indian uprisings. Because numerous crossings of the Naches River were required and the Pyramid area problem, this route fell into disuse after 1884, abandoned for lower and easier crossings. The original Naches Pass trail still winds through heavily wooded areas

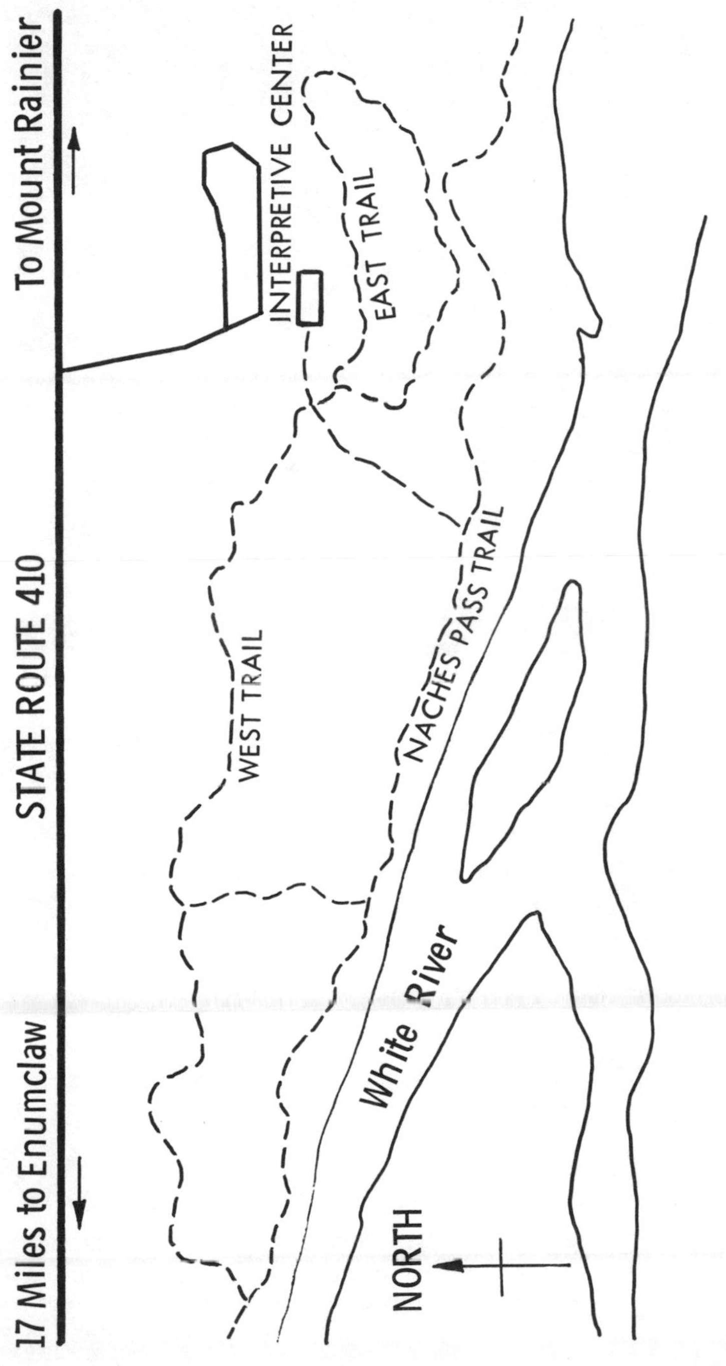
To Mount Rainier
STATE ROUTE 410
17 Miles to Enumclaw
INTERPRETIVE CENTER
EAST TRAIL
WEST TRAIL
NACHES PASS TRAIL
White River
NORTH
Federated Forest State Park

Pioneer Naches Pass wagon train trail winds through heavy timber and average underbrush much as it was originally cut through in 1853.
Author photo

Looking east on Highway 410, entrance to Federated Forest State Park is on the right.
Author photo

and summit meadows affording today's trail hiker the identical landscapes that were seen by pioneer wagon train groups. Spectacular views of Mount Rainier can be seen here.

Tree blazes made in the 1850s occasionally are found along this trail but only on larger standing trees. It is reported that the military used their own blaze. The one used by General McClelland consisted of an X with two bars below it. Most of these blazes have been obliterated by heavy bark growth.

Today part of the Federated Forest State Park west trail follows the original Naches Pass pioneer covered wagon road, some of which is still visible. Because this is a relatively short hike, it appeals to many senior-citizen and garden groups.

The trails in this park are level and easily can be walked. No special gear is required. This forest area is at foothill elevation, 20 miles north of Mount Rainier in the heart of the Cascades and alongside the White River.

An impressive interpretive center is located in the SE 612 acres of virgin timber. Of special note to those interested in plant life of Washington, exhibits can be seen that deal with the coast-forest zone,

Looking east towards Naches Peak at Chinook Pass near where Pacific Crest Trail crosses Highway 410.

Author photo

mountain-forest zone, sub-alpine zone, alpine zone, yellow pine forest zone, bunchgrass zone and sagebrush zone. Also featured are living displays that contain representative samples of plant life found in the first five listed zones.

To get to the Federated Forest from Seattle, drive east on Interstate 90. About one mile past Mercer Island, turn south on Interstate 405. Go seven miles, and take Exit 4 in Renton. Join State Route 169 and go left (east) 19 miles to Enumclaw. Here turn left (east) on State Route 164 for about one-half mile and join State Route 410 going east. Drive 17 miles, and turn right at the Federated Forest State Park sign.

FORT CASEY — coastal defense artillery fort on Whidbey Island.

Round trip: 3 miles; allow full morning or afternoon.
High point: 100 feet.
Elevation gain: 100 feet.
Packed dirt paths and gravel beach.
Open year-round.

Hiking, historical browsing and beachcombing all are combined in this half-day hike at an isolated, long-since-deactivated fort. The Fort Casey trail in Washington is unique in that one may examine the only disappearing-carriage artillery coastal defense guns remaining in the United States. After the Spanish American War in 1898, the War Department

Fort Casey

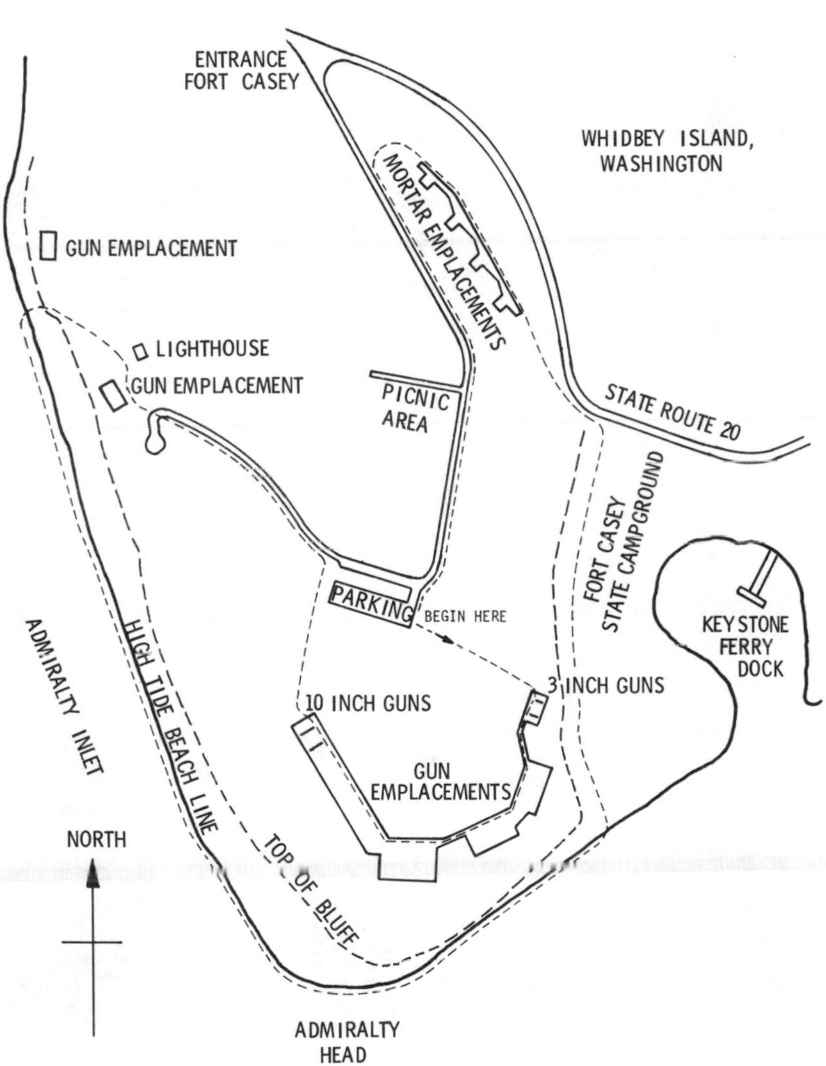
ENTRANCE
FORT CASEY
WHIDBEY ISLAND,
WASHINGTON
MORTAR EMPLACEMENTS
GUN EMPLACEMENT
LIGHTHOUSE
GUN EMPLACEMENT
PICNIC
AREA
STATE ROUTE 20
FORT CASEY
STATE CAMPGROUND
PARKING
BEGIN HERE
KEY STONE
FERRY
DOCK
ADMIRALTY INLET
HIGH TIDE BEACH LINE
3 INCH GUNS
10 INCH GUNS
GUN
EMPLACEMENTS
NORTH
TOP OF BLUFF
ADMIRALTY
HEAD

One of the former Fort Casey headquarters buildings constructed in 1898.

Author photo

The now decommissioned Admiralty Head lighthouse is the park's interpretive center. The light marked the entrance to Admiralty Inlet and Puget Sound to the south.

Author photo

Closeup of a ten-inch disappearing artillery rifle coastal defense gun in the extended ready-to-fire position. After each shell was fired the rifle was retracted for reloading. The hiking trail goes by two such guns formerly used to defend Puget Sound.
Author photo

authorized the establishment of three coastal artillery posts for the defense of Puget Sound. The defense perimeter included the Navy Yard at Bremerton and the cities of Seattle, Olympia, Everett and Tacoma.

In addition to Fort Casey, artillery posts were constructed at Fort Flagler and Fort Warden, strategically located across Admiralty Inlet so that no enemy vessel could escape the fire of their guns. These fortifications were extensive. Fort Casey had 10 batteries with a total of 25 guns ranging from 12-inch mortars and 10-inch rifles on disappearing carriages to smaller, rapid-firing guns on pedestals. Large guns mounted on disappearing carriages were a characteristic feature of early coastal forts. Guns of this type were withdrawn behind a thick concrete parapet after each round was fired.

Fort Casey was officially activated in 1900 and remained an integral part of the United States' defense until 192l, when it was placed on caretaker status. Although its guns were never fired in anger, its facilities were used extensively, mainly in the summer months by the ROTC, Washington National Guard and the U. S. Army Reserve personnel.

One will find on the fort grounds old, stately looking quarters of the post—barracks, officers' quarters, command headquarters, parade grounds—plus such other functional buildings as were required of a Victorian-era military post. Some of these buildings now are used by Seattle Pacific College. The trail, which leads past the gun emplace-

View looking north of Fort Casey parade ground and headquarters buildings with coastal defense gun emplacement in foreground. Driftwood strewn beach borders Admiralty Inlet.

Robert E. Oestreich photo

ments and the old Admiralty Inlet lighthouse and finishes with a beach hike, mixes history with the solitude of a delightful beachcombing walk. What better way to contemplate northwest military history during the end of the nineteenth century?

From the parking lot head southeast to the far end of the gun emplacements. Each battery was named for a war hero, most of them from the Spanish-American War. Walk the horseshoe-shaped line of batteries ending with the two 10-inch rifle guns, one extended and one retracted. Proceed north to the old Admiralty Head lighthouse, now an information center showing artifacts and historic development of the fort. Be sure to view the Fresnel lens system of the lighthouse (it originally used kerosene lamps).

From the lighthouse, drop down to the beach on the easy trail and head to the left, or south. Here you are apt to have the whole beach to yourself. This leads to Admiralty Head, the southernmost tip of the fort. Continue around in a northeasterly direction to the Fort Casey State Campground. Walk past the campground and take the path that leads up the hill to the mortar installations. Another left takes you back to the parking area.

Watch for wildlife, especially rabbits and hawks. The flora includes goldenrod, Michaelmas daisy, spirea, salal, Oregon grape and, of course, the beautiful evergreens.

The weather in this area is generally mild in all seasons. The rainfall is a mere 15 inches per year due to the fort's location in Washington's "banana belt," an area in the lee of the Olympic Mountains on which most of the Pacific Ocean's wet air has been deposited as rain or snow.

To get to Fort Casey from Seattle, Washington, drive north on Interstate 5 about 20 miles. At exit 187 bear right at the Mukilteo Whidbey Island Ferry sign. Join State Route 526 West on the overpass heading west. After 3.5 miles from Interstate 5 the Boeing 747 Jumbojet final assembly plant—the largest building ever built—looms to the right. At 2 more miles turn right, or north, at a traffic light onto State Route 525 to the Mukilteo ferry landing. The Washington State Ferry System has service to Whidbey Island most of the year on a half-hour departure schedule.

After a 20-minute ride, the ferry debarks at Columbia Beach on Whidbey Island. Continue on Route 525 for 23 miles. En route you pass scenic Greenbank, where an extensive loganberry vineyard is located. At milepost 30 turn left, or west, onto State Route 20, and sign also pointing to the Keystone Ferry. Go 6 miles past low sand dunes, the Keystone Ferry dock and the Fort Casey State Campground, all on the left. The entrance to Fort Casey is a short distance beyond, also on the left.

The fort is open from 6:30 a.m. to 10 p.m. except Mondays and Tuesdays, when it is closed. A picnic area with running water is provided. The fort visit with its amenities will be pleasant even if you do not take the full trail hike. For the hike carry canteen and camera.

HIRAM M. CHITTENDEN LOCKS — the western United States' largest and busiest ship locks.

One way: 2 miles; allow one hour one way.
Flat terrain. Easy afternoon walk on piers, gravel, and pavement.
Open year-round.

Started in 1916, two years after the opening of the Panama Canal, the Chittenden Locks in Washington serve vessels of all sizes, from small outboard boats to ocean-going cargo ships, during continuous night and day operations.

These locks were named in honor of the U. S. Army Corps of Engineers' district engineer and principal designer. They are popularily known as "Government" or "Ballard" locks, the latter being from Seattle.

These locks consist of a vertical-lift waterway traffic revision that provides access for commercial ships and pleasure boats alike between Puget Sound and Lake Union. Thanks to two man-made canals, a whole system of bays and lakes are interconnected with the locks. This vast waterway system has stimulated the impetus for the Seattle Region being America's largest boat ownership per capita.

Hiram M. Chittendon Locks

About a mile east of the locks, the Port of Seattle Fisherman's Terminal is at the south end of Salmon Bay. A large fleet of fishing vessels is berthed here. Our trail starts at this wharf, proceeds along the Salmon Bay Canal and ends at the locks.

What makes this trail so special is its variety. It is a good opportunity to visit the wharf with all of its activities, to hike along a portion of the ship canal, to see spawning salmon heading for fresh water at the underwater fish ladder, to walk across the ship canal lock gates and to enjoy lanscaped gardens adjoining the administration building. This multi-faceted trail thus is in marked contrast to most trails, which by their nature are single-purpose. On this trail there is something for almost anyone's interest.

We begin at Fisherman's Terminal, where over 1000 vessels will tie up during the fishing season. Often many kinds of fishing gear will be spread out for repair—gill nets, trolling gear, crabpots and buoys of all kinds add color to this scene. Large and small fishing vessels can be viewed from the 10 piers that extend from the wharf and net-storage sheds. To browse and enjoy the activity here is paramount on this trail. You may find so much that it will be hard to leave.

Part of the salmon fishing fleet that is tied up at Fisherman's Terminal. Purse seine net and reel on stern of seiner boat is shown in foreground.

Author photo

Boat traffic being lowered in the small lock serving commercial fishing and private pleasure craft. Levels of the water within the locks are controlled from operations station at the right.

Author photo

Spillway dam gates regulate height of fresh water behind locks for Lake Union and Lake Washington's huge inland waterway system. The connecting ramp to the underwater fish ladder viewing room is seen in the foreground.

Author photo

Placid dockside scene at Salmon Bay Fisherman's Terminal of hundreds of fishing boats, part of the salmon fishing fleet tied up here.

Author photo

From the wharf area proceed west and north past the restaurant onto West Commodore Way. This road parallels the east-west marine traffic through the locks. Walk about 1¼ miles to the locks. You will pass several marine industrial and construction yards. On the right is the U. S. Coast Guard Station. The new fish ladder building at the south end of the locks appears to the right.

At the fish ladder proceed down the steps to the underwater viewing room. This ladder is a series of pools and falls that lead, staircase fashion, to the higher, fresh-water level. The windows alongside allow you to see the salmon swimming in an almost stationary position against the water flowing past the windows. Here several species of salmon are visible at the same time, some as big as 30 pounds and as long as three feet. In the fall, fisheries' representatives identify fish here at the ladder by manually attaching small metal tags to their upper fins as part of their research on the habits of the fish.

Beyond is the spillway dam with its six gates. More salmon may be seen here, milling around in the water in front of the spillway dam awaiting Mother Nature's signal to begin their final dash to the spawning beds. Gates of the long spillway dam control the level of the water at the upper side for the ship canal, Lake Union, Portage Bay and Lake Washington.

Past the dam we can walk onto the two locks where the drop in water levels are dramatically evident during operation. On one side the level is just under our feet; at the other it is 25 feet lower. The southern lock is shorter and narrower and is intended for use by smaller vessels. The main lock parallels this one immediately to the north. Here large ships, tugs pulling log booms, sailboats, fishing boars and expensive yachts are typical traffic that may be seen nearly any hour of any day. Average time for passage through the larger lock is 25 minutes; through the small, 10 minutes. No charge is made for any vessel using this facility.

Seven acres of lawns and botanic gardens containing flowers, trees and shrubs from many lands are on display on the administration building grounds. The government horticulturist exchanges seeds with others all over the world to provide continual updating of the gardens, which attract visiting botanists from many countries.

The main entrance to the locks complex is at this garden plot, which faces NW Market Street. Visiting hours for the locks are 7 a.m. to 9 p.m. daily.

To approach the starting point of this trail from downtown Seattle, head north along the waterfront on Alaskan Way. At about one mile, take a one block jog to the right and then left onto Elliott Avenue. Proceed north about 1¼ miles, meeting 15th Avenue West. Go another 1¼ miles and turn right at the Emerson Street exit sign, but continue with a 270-degree turn to the west over 15th Avenue West to the stop sign at Emerson Street. Turn left and proceed on Emerson Street about

1 ¼ mile and turn right at entrance to Fisherman's Terminal and parking area. Don't forget your camera.

LOST CREEK RIDGE TRAIL — a spectacular mountain in North Cascades.

One way: 5 miles; allow 4 hours one way.
High point: 3550 feet.
Mountainous and rugged.
Strenuous hike with considerable elevation gain.
Open late summer depending on the previous winter snow.

My purpose in suggesting this hike is to give you an opportunity to climb to a vantage point on Lost Creek Ridge so that you can see and photograph a striking profile of Sloan Peak. Few mountains are as unique or as photgenic as 7790 Sloan Peak, with its monk's hood appearance. Two additional pleasures on this trail are the ability to view 10,540-foot, snow-covered Glacier Peak, to the northeast and, conditions permitting, the chance to visit Round Lake, to the north.

Because of the elevation, location and lengthy snow season, it is best to check ahead with the Forest Service. From the crest of the Lost Creek Ridge trail, the side trail to Round Lake leads down steep slopes to the lake but is hazardous in snow. This side trail does not melt until late summer.

Switchbacks on trail up steep slope to Bingley Gap proceed through thick open woods.
Carol Severson photo

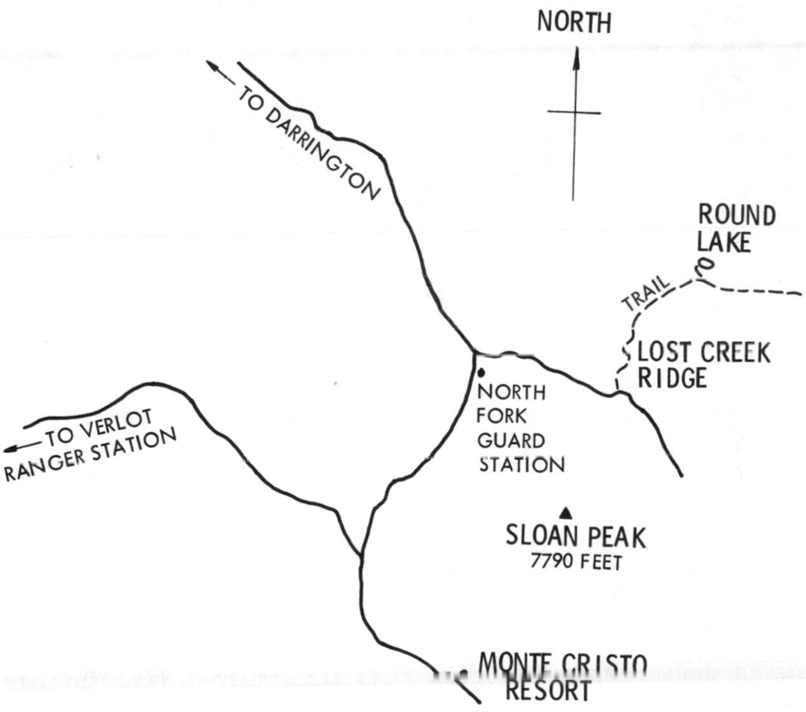

Lost Creek Ridge Trail

A brief opening in the clouds provides shadow contrast across glacier field on easily identified Sloan Peak as viewed from Lost Creek Ridge trail.
Barbara Newell photo

Many people enjoy this hike as a day trip for its outstanding vistas. For overnight backpackers, the trail continues on to Kennedy Hot Springs, with its warm bath, and finishes on the White Chuck River Road. Taking this route requires being met at the end in several days. It is a 19-mile hike from one road to the other.

Lost Creek Ridge Trail is located in the Mount Baker National Forest, 30 miles east of the Verlot Ranger station, or about 15 miles southwest of Darrington. Taking this trail will give you access to the Glacier Peak Wilderness. The Cascade Crest Trail passes between Sloan Peak and Glacier Peak.

The trail begins on the Sloan Creek road, number 308, about 3½ miles east of its junction with the Darrington-Monte Cristo Road. At the left is parking and a trail sign. After about ½ mile of easy trail, it rises steeply with continuous switchbacks through open woods. In three miles it rises 2425 feet to Bingley Gap. Along this portion of the trail are open views of Sloan Peak. Here you may want to stop and take pictures of this impressive peak. From Bingley Gap the trail continues another 2 miles along the ridge to a saddle where Round Lake is viewed to the left, or north. The short ¼ mile side trip into Round Lake is recommended only when the snow has melted. East of the saddle are good views of Sloan Peak and Glacier Peak. Here is where your telephoto lens comes in handy.

Round Lake as viewed from summit of Lost Creek Ridge trail. Hike into this lake should not be attempted until snow is melted.

Carol Severson photo

In August there still may be snow on the ridge. In overcast conditions, be prepared for chilly weather and cold winds. When planning this hike, try for a sunny day. Your black and white and color pictures of photogenic Sloan Peak, taken either in the morning or afternoon, will be among your very favorites of the Washington Cascades. Incidentally, renown hiking and mountaineering photographers Bob and Ira Spring—who, with Harvey Manning, did the classic *101 Hikes in the North Cascades* —chose for their cover a photograph of Sloan Peak taken from the Lost Creek Ridge Trail.

To get to the Lost Creek Ridge trail from Seattle, drive north on Interstate 5 about 30 miles to Everett. Take exit 194 and Route 2 east for three miles, and turn left on Route 204 toward Granite Falls. In 2½ miles turn left (north) on Route 92 at the stoplight. After 1½ miles turn right (east). Mount Pilchuck looms directly ahead. At the town of Granite Falls proceed ahead, after a four-way stop, three short blocks to the second stop sign. Turn left on South Alder way past the high school on the right toward Verlot.

Upon entering Mount Baker National Forest, the Verlot Ranger Station is at another ¼ mile. Stop at the Ranger Station to check snow conditions and obtain a permit for overnight camping. The road is paved for the next 20 miles east of Verlot to Barlow Pass. Here turn left (north) onto Darrington—Monte Cristo road for about 7 miles past the North Fort Guard Station on the right to Sloan Creek road, number 308, also on the right. As indicated, the trail is 3½ miles in and on the left.

This trail provides a variety of closed and open woods, open meadows, a crest-ridge view of mountain peaks and good picture taking. The 3550 foot climb in five miles is well worth the effort, especially if you bring both cameras. Pictures of Sloan Peak will impress your friends.

MAIDEN OF THE WOODS — a super wood carving.

One way: ¾ mile; allow 2 hours.
Interesting half day hike.
Good in any season.
Wide trail and easy grade.

Nowhere else in the Pacific Northwest will you find so large a wood sculpture on a cedar tree. Part of this tremendous tree is dead, part of it is still alive. What attracts hikers to its base is the 16-foot high carved form of a woman leaning against its trunk. This tree, named Maiden of the Woods by the U.S. Forest Service, is located in a primitive forest.

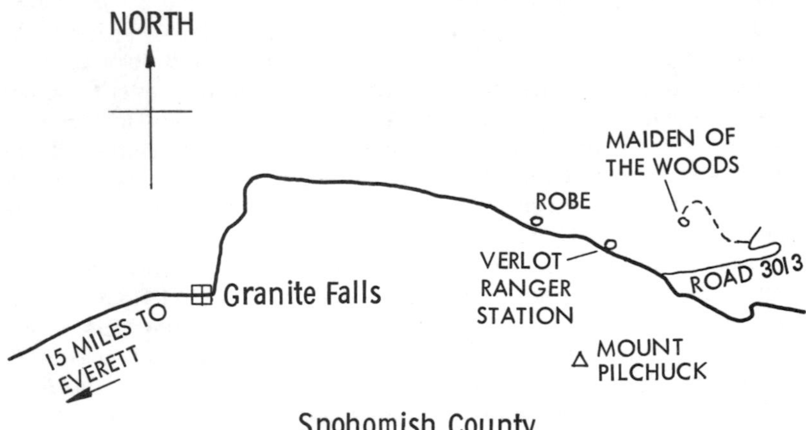

Maiden of the Woods

Maiden-of-the woods as seen from below with part of staging still attached at the left of the tree trunk.
Author photo

Forest Service Road 3013 bears left as viewed a short distance east of Verlotte general store on Granite Falls-Monte Cristo Road in Mount Baker National Forest.

Author photo

Sculptors conjure up great ideas. South Dakota's Gutzon Borglum conceived the great Mount Rushmore. Washington's Dudley Carter created a masterpiece.

In 1947 wood sculptor Carter, using only an ax, began the figure of the woman. The woman was to have been the main figure of the group, but she is now only partially complete. He planned to portray animals, birds and wood life farther up the trunk. Carter considers finishing the figure, but question of tree ownership may be troublesome since it now may be part of government land.

The sculpture is about 25 miles east of Everett, Washington, in the Mount Baker National Forest. It is located on a trail that begins on a park service road that is past the community of Verlot. The trail's relatively short length, width and grade make for an easy afternoon walk.

Much of the trail is through a primitive forest, where one might see visionary maidens, wood spirits and animals. Occasional alder thickets contrast with the predominent large and somber conifer growth.

We marveled at cedar stumps of immense proportions. Ahead is a huge cedar tree with a massive trunk. The many burls near its tremendous root base attract our attention. Suddenly around on the west side of the trunk we see the outline of a figure in the sunlight. Upon walking a few feet to the right to get a better view of the maiden, we found that the trail had ended.

The winsome carved maiden slowly begins to captivate us. Here is modern day art applied in Haida Indian totem style but on a much larger scale. We find we cannot back far enough into the woods to get a good picture of it. It slowly dawns on us that there is live growth on this tree. The upper jagged portion indicates that the tree was hit in a monumental lightning strike or had been carried away in some violent windstorm. Symbolism has been added by nature.

Plan on staying a while to enjoy the various patterns made by light and shadows. She captures the afternoon sun. Noon to mid-afternoon is best for photographs.

We went hiking immediately after the snow had melted and had the privilege of making the year's first footprints. A winter washout on the road kept us from our destination, but it added favorably to the pleasure of the hike. We heard winter wrens and flushed a grouse.

To get there from Seattle, take Interstate 5 north 30 miles to Everett. At exit 194 take Route 2 on the raised highway east over lowlands. At three miles turn left on Route 204 east toward Granite Falls. In 2½ miles, turn left (north) on Route 92 at the stoplight. After 1½ miles turn right (east). Here Mount Pilchuck looms directly ahead. At Granite Falls proceed ahead, after the four-way stop, three short blocks to second stop sign. Turn left (north) onto South Alder Way, toward Verlot, the high school is on the right. Part of the way, the drive runs along the south fork of the Stillaguamish River and through second-growth evergreen trees.

Upon entering Mount Baker National Forest, the Ranger Station is about ¼ mile in on the left. Soon the Verlot general store appears on the right. Beyond the store prepare to bear left at Road 3013. In about 1½ miles the road makes a sharp hairpin to the left and up a steeper grade. Here past a road sign reading Dead End Service Road, about 100 yards ahead, the trail takes off to the left after a right hand turn. The trail is marked by a post on the right. Carry water and camera.

In this immediate area and within a radius of 17 miles, there are 39 additional hikes of varying distance and difficulty listed in the Monte Cristo Ranger District Trail Guide. You could spend most of a summer hiking the trails right here.

MIMA MOUNDS — one million eerie, historical mounds.

Round trip: 200 yards to two miles; allow one to four hours.
High point: elevation gain zero.
Good any season; spring is delightful.
Pasture with bunch grass, black soil with gravel near surface, thick woods.
Open all year.

There may be no other hiking area in the world quite like the unusual Mima Mounds. One million earth mounds, all about the same size, looking like giant molehills, extend in a continual, regular pattern over an area of approximately 80 square miles. Through some fluke of

Mima Mounds

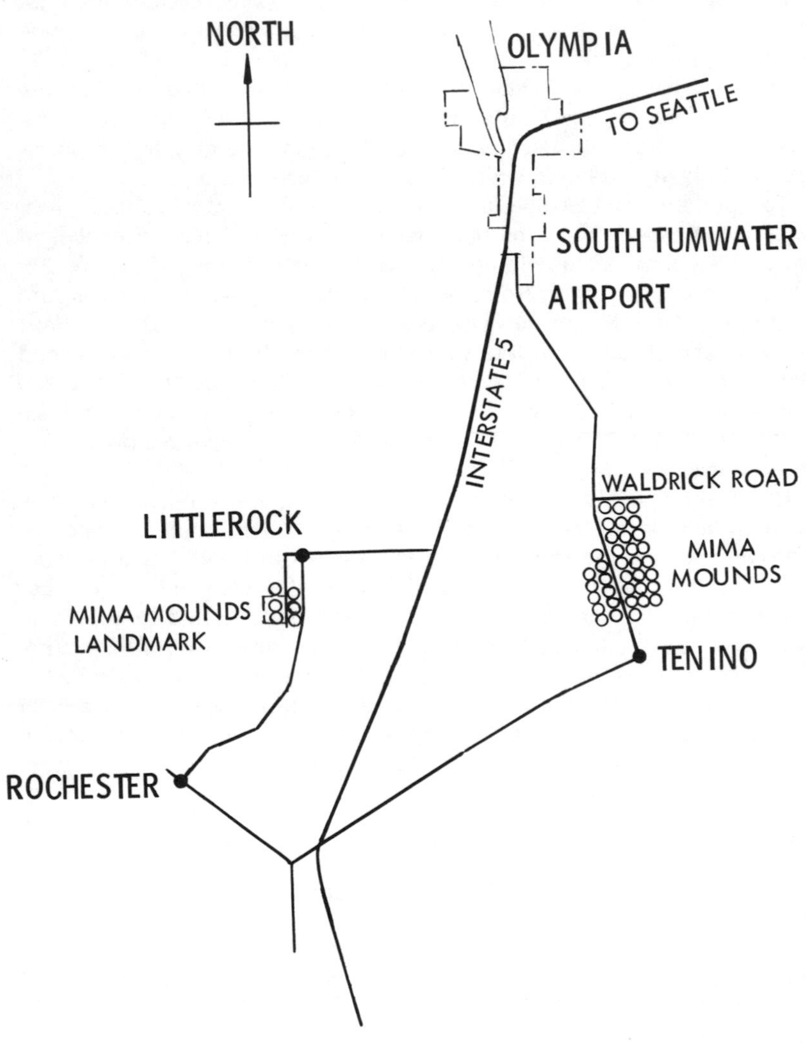
NORTH
OLYMPIA
TO SEATTLE
SOUTH TUMWATER
AIRPORT
INTERSTATE 5
WALDRICK ROAD
LITTLEROCK
MIMA MOUNDS
MIMA MOUNDS LANDMARK
TENINO
ROCHESTER

At Mima Mounds site near Walrick Road north of Tenino, Washington. Telegraph poles in background show location of sunken railroad grade.
Author photo

Mother Nature in a region near Tenino, Washington, there are acres after acres of hillocks from 2 to 7 feet high and 10 to 30 feet in diameter rising from the broad table terrain south of Olympia. To hike this area is to walk *through* the areas of these mounds, not necessarily up, down and across them. Much of this region, named for the Mima Prairie, is pasture land with low bunch grass containing many wildflowers; in the summer one hears the songs of meadowlarks.

At first glance these mounds appear to be manmade, but soon their vast dispersion almost defies imagination. Much of this hummock-marked land is now fenced and used as pasture. The soil cover is dark in color and rich in appearance. The subsoil turns quickly to gravel; several commercial shallow gravel pits skirt the area. Portions of this region are now forested, appearing to have been seeded after the mounds were formed. Thus, these mounds continue their almost regular pattern in the shadow of random but thick fir growth.

As to the creation of these mounds, biologists, geologists and rank amateurs alike have propounded theories—but no single one advanced so far has cleared up the mystery. Some of the theories make for remarkable reading—burial grounds, volcanic hives, gophers, root structures or buffalo mounds.

Roadway Marker on south side of Registered Natural Landmark area relates that Mima Mounds are a geologic mystery. The configuration of these mounds is seen to the left of the marker.

Author photo

The probable origin of these mounds has been a continual source of interest to geologists and others for at least 130 years. The burial ground theory does not match the estimated population settlements prior to 1846. One recent theory is that when the region was subjected to ice and glacial climate, the ground surfaces exhibited a "permafrost" condition as is experienced in Alaska and other arctic regions. This combined with the southbound runoff of the Vashon Glacier then covering the Puget South region may have interacted in a fashion to create sedimentary ripples in the earth. Such ridges, hills or mounds of stratified drift deposited by glacial runoff are known as *kames*.

But there is no agreement on their formation. The region is underlaid by Vashon gravel. However, the mounds themselves are composed of black, pebbly silt and sand that overlay the gravel outwash. This might indicate that the Mima Mounds were deposited at this location through some unusual hydraulic and meteorological turbulence conditions.

To get to one of the more northerly sites, drive south on Interstate 5 from Olympia. At South Tumwater take exit 102 marked South Tumwater and Black Lake. At the stoplight turn left, and proceed over Interstate 5. One block beyond, this street becomes Trosper Road. At the next stop sign turn south, following the sign to Tenino. This street marked Capitol Boulevard is actually Old 99 Highway. Drive about eight miles, first passing the airport on the right, to Waldrick Road on the left and turn left. Soon turn right onto a dirt road which parallels the sunken railroad right-of-way. The mounds appear to the south and southeast from this vantage point.

To visit the National Registry of Historic Places listed Mima Mounds Landmark region, which is some distance west from the first sighting, drive south about five miles to Tenino. Along this road on both sides more mounds can be seen in the open or wooded tracts. From Tenino travel west about seven miles, cross over Interstate 5, join State Route 12 and drive five miles to Rochester, turning right, or north, onto State Route 121. Drive six miles to the junction at Little Rock and turn left, or west, toward the *Gate* across a rail track and over a creek, then up a small hill in the woods bearing left, or south, for 1¼ miles. To the immediate right is a barbed wire cattle gate and a No Vehicles sign on the fence. This is an entrance to the Mima Mounds Landmark, an area extending perhaps a half-mile westward and as much north and south.

To view the official roadway marker drive another 1/10 mile south and turn west onto Bordeaux Road. The marker appears on the right about a quarter mile distant, along the south border of the Landmark.

Looking across thousands of mounds and the Black Hills region to the northeast, one does wonder what prior geologic glacial turn of events created this huge settling basin—one full of mounds about 10 miles in both directions, between the Deschutes and Skookumchuck Rivers—for all to marvel at and be mystified by.

To return along a more direct route to Interstate 5, retrace your steps to Little Rock but continue east on 121 three miles to Interstate 5. If this landmark is your prime ofjective and you are traveling south on 5, the turn to Little Rock to the west is Exit 95.

Here is one strange hiking area—one you will never forget.

OZETTE LAKE — the site of the Pacific Coast's outstanding archaeological dig.

One way: 3 miles each leg; allow one day.
High point: 100 feet.
Elevation loss: 100 feet.
Easy day hike or overnight backpack.
Open all year-round.

This Olympic National Park coast trial is shaped like an equilateral triangle, with each side being about three miles long. The first tip of the triangle is at the trailhead near the Ozette Lake Ranger Station. A second tip is at Sand Point on a secluded Pacific Ocean beach. The third tip also is along the ocean shoreline at Cape Alava and marks the location of the Ozette Village dig, one of the most, if not *the* most significant archaeological finds in all of North America.

Campsites are available at Cape Alava. There are also seasonal guided tours of this site, since it was an Indian village that was covered

Hiker almost becomes lost in root layout of stump washed ashore on Pacific Ocean beach near Cape Alava.

Dave Smith photo

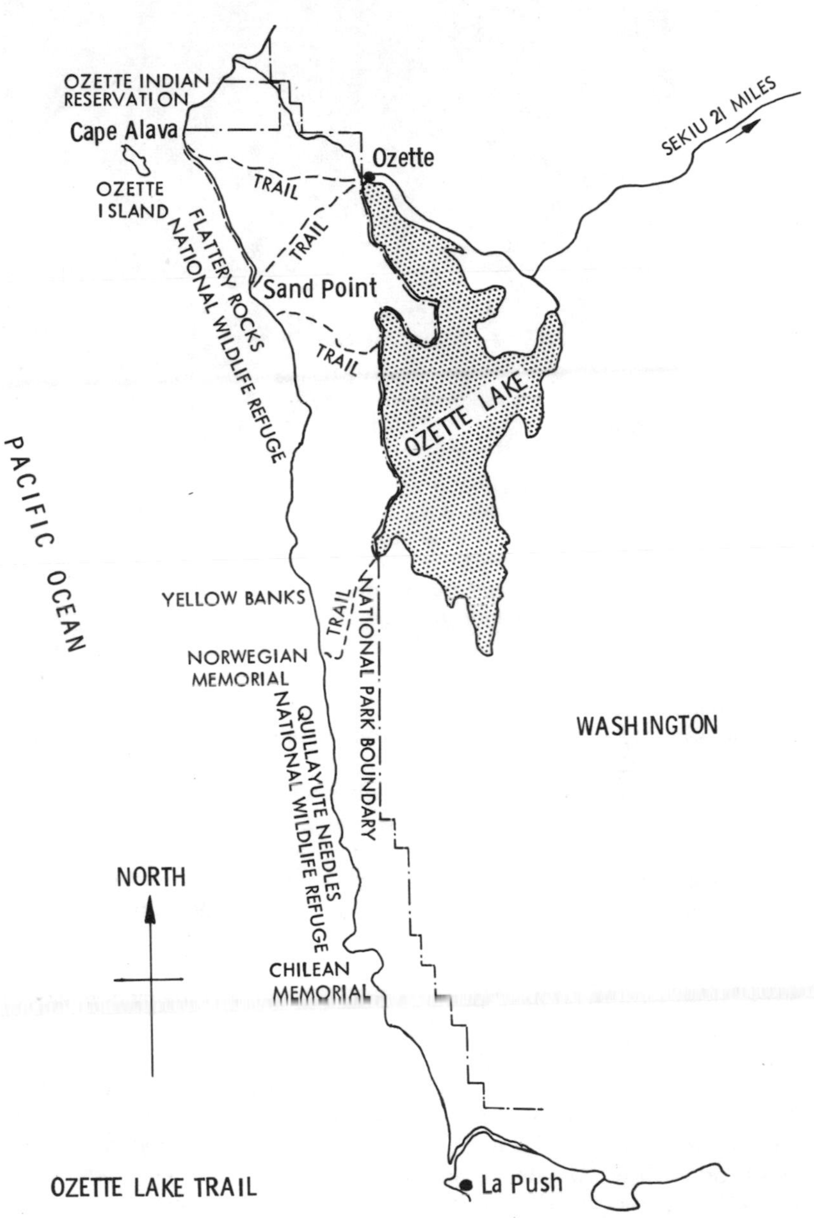
OZETTE INDIAN RESERVATION
Cape Alava
OZETTE ISLAND
Ozette
SEKIU 21 MILES
TRAIL
TRAIL
FLATTERY ROCKS NATIONAL WILDLIFE REFUGE
Sand Point
TRAIL
OZETTE LAKE
PACIFIC OCEAN
YELLOW BANKS
TRAIL
NATIONAL PARK BOUNDARY
NORWEGIAN MEMORIAL
QUILLAYUTE NEEDLES NATIONAL WILDLIFE REFUGE
WASHINGTON
NORTH
CHILEAN MEMORIAL
OZETTE LAKE TRAIL
La Push

Ozette Lake

At the beach end of the Lake Ozette hiking trail is the Cape Alava archaeological dig under the direction of Washington State University. Historic Indian village was covered by slide from clay bank and preserved for hundreds of years. Many artifacts are still being uncovered here.

Dave Smith photo

by mudslides and hermetically sealed for 500 years. The dig has been ongoing since the late 1960s under the direction of Washington State University experts.

Over 40,000 artifacts have been recovered and catalogued. Conical rain hats, baskets, mats, combs, knives and canoe paddles have been unearthed. There are finely-worked halibut hooks and wooded seal oil bowls, with decorative carving. Rope, harpoons, points and other gear used by ancient Indians for hunting seals and whales, that migrated past Cape Alava, indicate the lifestyle of these early people. Five years ago a magnificent whale carving was found on a 17-foot-long cedar plank, used as a decorative panel in the longhouse. After two weeks of careful work, the plank was lifted out of the mud and there were more articles under it—a bowl, shell beads still strung together and a beautifully carved loom. All this represents the opening of a time capsule containing the culture of the Ozette Indian tribe. Many of the artifacts will be stored at Neah Bay at the new museum and cultural center. These artifacts will be staying in the same area where they were found and will be cared for by descendants of the Ozette People.

The hiker of this trip has several options—a day hike into the dig, an overnight at Sand Point or a beach hike south from Sand Point and back for an easy second overnight.

Both trails, the Indian Village Nature trail to Cape Alava and the

Youthful backpacking hikers find scenic tentsite on shore of Pacific Ocean at end of Cape Alava beach trail.

Lyn Watts photo

Sand Point trail, start from the trailhead at Ozette Lake. Both go through a typical, quiet oceanside forest on improved trails, parts of which are cedar plank walkways raised above the wet marshy areas. The trails usually are maintained very well. Waterproof footwear is a must, especially in damp weather. A friend of mine recently jogged all the way out without stopping. The only reason he didn't jog back was because he had to carry all the beachcombed items that he found.

This Pacific Ocean beach area is relatively isolated. There is a beach trail south, but the nearest road access is 18 miles away at La Push. Thus you will see no tire tracks, nor hordes of people digging clams, surf fishing or looking for oriental tidbits in the driftwood. It is one of the few Pacific Ocean beaches truly to be enjoyed by the hiker and backpacker. For this privilege we are grateful to those who prepared this strip as a portion of the Olympic National Park.

To get to Ozette Lake from downtown Seattle, take the 45-minute ferry trip across Elliott Bay and Puget Sound to Winslow, Bainbridge Island. Follow State Route 305 across the island and the Agate Pass Bridge where you join State Route 3 and, farther, 104 when you cross the Hood Canal Floating Toll Bridge. Join State Route 101 past Sequim to Port Angeles—a total distance of 78 miles. Here take State Route 112 to Sekiu, another 49 miles. About 3 miles past Sekiu turn left (south) onto the well-marked road to Ozette Lake, a distance of 21 miles. When approaching the lake, bear right. The Ozette Lake Ranger Station and parking lot are at the end of the road.

The Indian Village Nature Trail to Cape Alava goes to the right. About half way out is Ahlstrom's Prairie, a former homestead farm clearing. After reaching the archaeological dig, you can walk north a short distance to nearby Indian Island to see the cannonball rocks at low tide. Petroglyphs can be inspected on the boulders at Ozette Village. The old anchor of the *Austria* lost in 1887, can also be seen at low tide near here. Going south, the three mile hike is mostly over beach cobble, while many huge boulders of varying sizes dot the ocean horizon with Ozette Island about a mile offshore. The Sand Point Trail is an even grade return to Ozette Lake.

Be prepared to see deer, elk, bear and small mammals such as raccoons. Waterfowl and birds can be found at the ends of trails. Although in spring there may be seasonably warm weather, expect the worst, and bring raingear at any season. Your tent must be waterproof, and be sure to bring a substantial groundcover. The annual rainfall exceeds 100 inches.

SKAGIT WILDLIFE RECREATION AREA — saltwater wildlife refuge.

Round trip: three miles; allow two hours.
Sea level walk across tidelands.
Easy half-day hike.
Open all year around.

There is no more memorable a hike than along a saltwater delta flyway area. To be able to experience the thrill of seeing thousands of migratory waterfowl line the sky is an incomparable hiking pleasure. Overhead one may see numerous V formations and other flocks resting on the water. To see the numerous flights of wintering snow geese—brilliant white with black wing tips contrasted against grey skies, taking to the air simultaneously with the water flapping and honking—is to enjoy one of life's greater adventures of the Pacific Northwest. Rare trumpeter and whistling swans also can be seen.

The Washington Game Department established the Skagit Wildlife Recreation Area on migratory waterfowl flyway lands so that the hiker and bird watcher can observe an array of wildlife every season. There are three classes of birds seen here: full-time residents, en route migrators and migrators that winter here.

Located on Fir Island in Skagit Bay, between the mouths of the north and south forks of the glacier-fed Skagit and Stillaguamish Rivers, the refuge encompasses tidal marsh land and diked crop lands. This area, which is in the lee of the Olympic Mountains, faces the saltwater reach between upper Whidbey Island and the mainland.

This hike can be taken by people of all ages. Most of the trail runs on the top of flood control dikes, which are land fills about eight feet

Skagit Wildlife Recreation Area

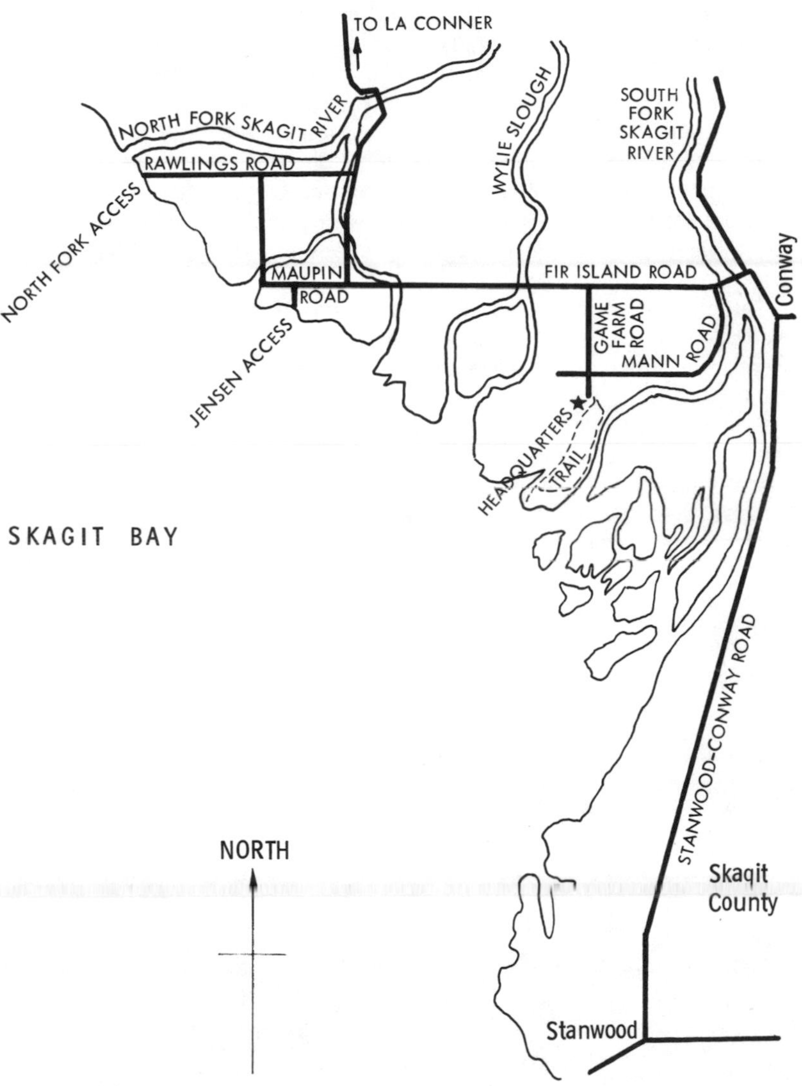

above high tide level and thirty feet wide and extend seaward across marsh land. The trail is convenient for both individual hikers and parties of watchers. Starting at the refuge headquarters, the trail consists of a large loop with two arms extending to the west at the far end. Other hiking and viewing sites are located in the area.

The weather here is generally moderate. The marsh land is extensive and exposed. For fall and winter hikes, prepare for chilling damp winds since there is no shelter here. Prevailing southwest Pacific Ocean winds produce snow on the Olympic Mountains en route to these flats. From the opposite direction, cool air from the east flows down the snowcapped Cascade Mountains and on nearby foothills. Plan on wearing wool clothes, with rain cover, for wind protection, even in overcast spring weather. Comfortable walking shoes are desired. Bring binoculars.

Cattails border the dikes and tidal marsh inlets. Wild parsnip, pearly everlasting, dock, scrub alder with lichen and moss, wild rose, and an occasional blue spruce accentuate the brush—all ideal cover for the wildlife.

Flocks of resident shorebirds frequent the area. Many bird species can be seen, depending on the season. Regarding birds that stay year-round, look for teal, wood duck, mallard, pheasant, killdeer, sandpiper, tanager, meadowlark, red-wing blackbird, towhee, wren, bush tit and kinglets. Migratory fowl include snow geese, green-wing teal, pintail,

Turn in for parking at Skagit Wilderness-Recreation Area. Hike goes along lowland saltwater flats where wildlife feed and have cover.

Author photo

Felled tree across slough provides easy bridge for bird watcher at Skagit River Wildlife-Recreation Area.

Author photo

baldpate and the occasional trumpeter and whistling swans. Birds of prey also are found here such as the bald eagle, duck hawk, cooper, sharpshin and red tail hawks and snowy owl.

Furbearing mammals also live in the refuge. Look for otter, muskrat, beaver, raccoon and skunk. Deer, salmon, steelhead and trout visit the refuge, again depending on the season. Huge blue heron stalk the banks of drainage ditches. Where else at the 48th latitude could you hear a tree toad in mid-January and find a 50 degree temperature? Everywhere we hear the call of waterfowl. Cultivated fields of corn and other crops help to attract birdlife to Fir Island.

To visit the refuge from Seattle, head north on Interstate 5. About 27 miles beyond Everett, take exit 221. At the stop sign turn left (west) on State Route 530. Immediately turn right into Conway on the Fir Island Road. A few blocks beyond the rail crossing and bridge, turn left (south) on Mann Road. Continue south along the dike for two miles to Game Farm Road. A left turn at the sign takes you to the refuge headquarters. The headquarters has excellent information concerning the refuge and a map that gives directions to the hiking areas.

After hiking the route past the headquarters, it is well worth the time to visit one of the other nearby viewing areas. The closest one is Jensen Access located by going north on Game Farm Road, then left (west) on Fir Island Road. After traveling about three miles on the Fir Island Road and at a point where this road makes a right turn to the north, go straight ahead onto Maupin Road for a half mile and turn left (south) at the Jensen Access sign. A few steps from the parking lot to

Skagit River flats and saltwater marshes provide ideal cover for waterfowl.

Author photo

the top of the dike affords good viewing across Skagit Bay, where many migratory waterfowl will be found. For the return trip home, head east toward Conway and Interstate 5.

This hiking area is yet another that has a special significance and provides a rare experience.

YELLOWSTONE ROAD — an imperiled brick ribbon of the old Seattle-Yellowstone Park Highway.

Round trip: 2½ miles; allow two hours.
Flat terrain.
Easy afternoon walk.
Open year-round.

The last remaining portion of the original Yellowstone Road is located just outside Redmond, Washington. When it was paved with red bricks in 1910, it was the only road from Seattle to Snoqualmie Pass. Now Snoqualmie Pass is on the main east-west interhighway system linking Seattle and Spokane. The old road went on to Yellowstone National Park from Snowqualmie Pass and, because of that popular tourist destination, the name remains to this day.

This narrow red brick road, just wide enough for two cars, provides better hiking than driving. It also carries fond memories for many people here in the Northwest of earlier family vacation expeditions in open touring automobiles to see Old Faithful and to stay in the Park Lodge. Flat tires every few hundred miles were commonplace, and radiators boiled over regularly on the numerous hill climbs. Luggage was carried on the running boards, and, for those who camped along the way, an extra car tent at night kept off the dew and the dust.

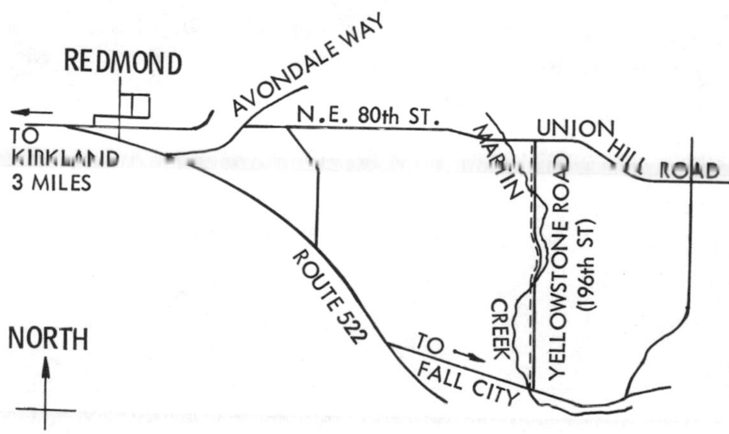

Yellowstone Road

View across brick road toward barn shows rural atmosphere of trail area.

Author photo

Farmhouse and garden border old Yellowstone Road with its red brick surface of antiquity.

Author photo

At south end of trail the brick pavement ends where a portion of the original road has been overlayed with asphalt.

Author photo

This short, flat stretch of brick road is about 1¼ miles long and has little traffic; thus it's an easy round-trip hike. The road passes through beautiful rural countryside that is dotted with old barns and fallen-in chicken houses. Portions of this road are shaded by firs and maples and are bounded by moss-covered rail fences. Sword fern, bracken and salal add to the flora.

Heading north through this pastoral scene we come to the wide flat valley of Martin Creek and its cattails. Only the muffled sounds of a nearby skeet and gun club are heard in the distance. Farther on are neat rural residences with picturesque namesigns. The trail and brick road end all too soon at NE 80th Street, also marked as Union Hill Road.

On the return walk we are reminded that this brick road is occasionally patched with asphalt overlays. The surface of the road shows tracks from wagon wheel and car tire wear, as would be expected after 66 years of continuous use. Most all brick roads have long since been repaved to eliminate their slippery surface condition during rain and frost. The road edge especially reveals its use and age, with intermittent layers of green moss attached to the cement grooves between the hard glazed surface of the bricks.

To find the Old Yellowstone Road when starting from Seattle, drive east on Interstate 90 over the world's busiest, if not the longest, concrete *caisson* floating bridge, then across Mercer Island and its East Channel bridge. After about seven miles from Seattle bear right to join Interstate 405 and go north. About nine miles farther turn right or east onto State Route 908 East and travel east about three miles to Redmond. Go through town and continue on State Route 202 East, which is also marked as the Redmond-Falls City Road, about two miles to 196th Street NE. Here turn left, or north, on this road and park about 200 yards ahead under fir trees where the red brick pavement is first visible.

On one of our hikes here we chatted with a young girl riding her horse, a bicycling family of six and others enjoying this ribbon in the countryside. All expressed their pleasure in passing over this charming road with its interesting history. Its principle charm lies in its roughness, narrowness, slipperiness when wet and general antiquity.

One final, important point. Visit this trail before it is too late. Through some accidental or misguided action, Federal Arterial Road Funds may be funneled to the county to repave this strip under the guise of road improvement. Should this happen, all evidence of the Old Yellowstone Road will be buried forever.

WELLINGTON — hike the region of the Great Northern Railroad avalanche disaster.

*Round Trip:*3 miles; allow 2 hours.
High Point: 3200 feet.
Easy half-day trip on old railroad bed.
Open June through October.
The word Wellington is well known to railroad men and connotes the world's worst avalanche railroad disaster of all time. This disaster took place on the Great Northern Railway mainline, high in the Cascade Mountains at Stevens Pass, near the exact center of Washington state. A thundering avalanche of snow rolled two trains down a mountainside taking the lives of 96 people; 40 people miraculously survived this terrible calamity.

During February 1910, in the midst of one of the nation's worst snow storms, railroad traffic in the Cascades almost stopped. At the 3100 foot elevation in Stevens Pass, two westbound Great Northern passenger and fast mail trains were halted at the rail yard of Wellington near the west end of the new 2½-mile long Cascade Tunnel. The cause was a series of snow slides about two miles west, at Windy Point. This exposed snowslideprone edge of Windy Mountain was a burned-over slope of tall snags that contained a snowfield rising 2000 feet to the top without a break. The unusually heavy snowfall was bad enough, but when moisture laden winds from the Pacific Ocean turned the snow into rain, there was real trouble.

Heavy, wet snows had built up on the steep slopes all along this particular trackage. Four rotary snowplows were dispatched to cut through the snowslides but were stopped by an avalanche at Windy Point. The 900-foot long and 25-feet high catastrophe effectively

Wellington

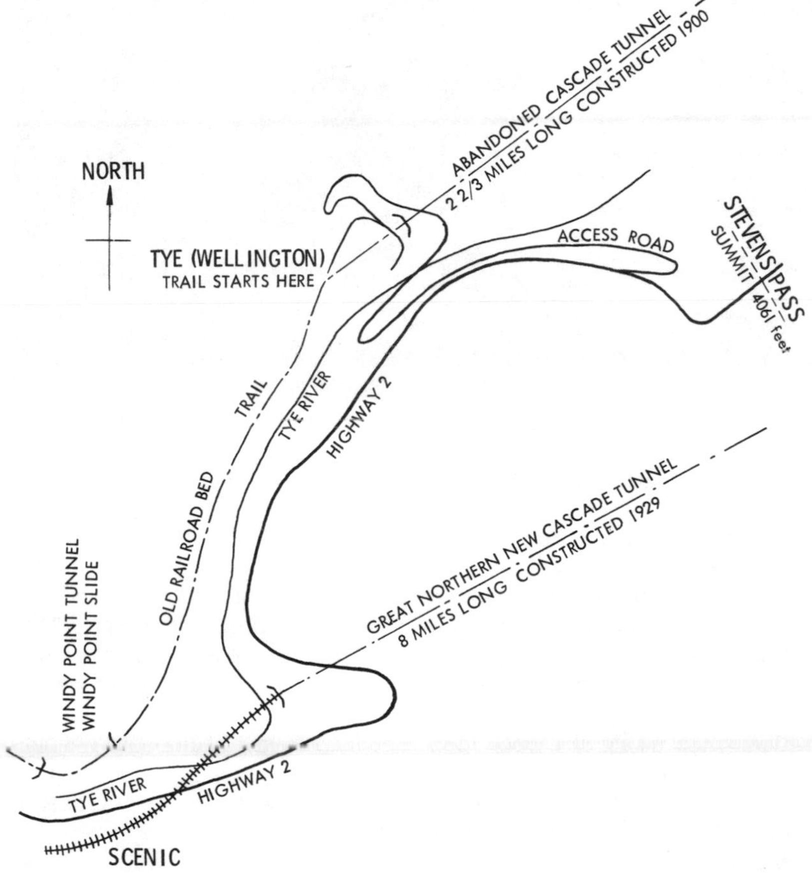
NORTH
ABANDONED CASCADE TUNNEL
2 2/3 MILES LONG CONSTRUCTED 1900
TYE (WELLINGTON)
TRAIL STARTS HERE
ACCESS ROAD
STEVENS PASS
SUMMIT 4061 feet
TRAIL
TYE RIVER
HIGHWAY 2
OLD RAILROAD BED
WINDY POINT TUNNEL
WINDY POINT SLIDE
GREAT NORTHERN NEW CASCADE TUNNEL
8 MILES LONG CONSTRUCTED 1929
TYE RIVER
HIGHWAY 2
SCENIC

This is the west portal of a 2½-mile-long tunnel also abandoned when rail line was rerouted to lower level.

The Wenatchee World photo

sealed off westbound travel. In a short time all four rotary snowplows were immobilized, while a second avalanche, east of Wellington, cut off the eastbound access. The snowplows could not cope with such conditions, including the stumps, rocks and logs embedded in the snow. The two trains standing at Wellington were trapped in snow that was almost as high as the railcars. Several days passed—the end nowhere in sight.

During the disastrous week food supplies ran low at the yard's small train crew hotel. Coal supplies for the locomotives were pinched. The trains had to be shuttled to the coal bunker and water tower in order to keep steam going and passenger cars heated.

March 1, on the eighth night, at 1 a.m., the snow field directly above the trains started to slide, triggered by an electrical storm. It became a giant avalanche that roared down the mountainside consuming everything. Both trains—locomotives and all—were hurled into the valley, splintering and tearing open passenger cars en route like so many toys. Of the 15 cars and six locomotives that had been in the yard, almost nothing visible remained. Everything within 1400 feet had been swept away.

To the right is abandoned railroad bed at Windy Point. Avalanche at this point prevented trains from proceeding west. Disaster occurred while trains were waiting for tracks ahead to be cleared.
Robert E. Oestreich photo

A train engineer, who happened to be outside, witnessed the disaster and immediately awakened other section yard people. They began the rescue, using lanterns to light their way. Only the end of one passenger car was sticking out of the debris in the valley below. The following day additional help hiked through deep snows to assist rescue teams. Not until eight days later was a train finally able to come in from the east, and transport the injured and dead.

The Great Northern Railroad, wanting to forget the memory, changed the name of the Yard at Wellington to Tye, after the river that ran through the adjoining valley to the south. Later, Windy Point was tunneled, and a mile of snowsheds were added from Wellington to Windy Point. At Wellington a 4000 foot long double-tracked snowshed of reinforced concrete was constructed. Nevertheless, the Great Northern management realized that its operations through Stevens Pass would have to be rerouted to a lower elevation. This meant going underground. So began the massive undertaking of a new $25 million tunnel and the rerouting of tracks 40 miles long. In 1929 this eight-mile tunnel was opened, which by-passed the entire Old Cascade Tunnel, Wellington Yard and Windy Point slide hazards. The old moss covered concrete snowshed at Tye still stands as a nomument to man's attempt to conquer winter Cascade Mountain snows—and to the Wellington dead.

The trail begins at Wellington and goes west along the old road bed. It first enters the concrete snowshed and proceeds for almost a mile under cover. It then follows along a high concrete retaining wall of almost the same length. Here the undergrowth gets thicker. Upon approaching Windy Point one is greeted by the 1200 foot long tunnel. From here a trail is planned to go down the steep hillside to the town of Scenic on the Stevens Pass Highway; however, trail easements have yet to be obtained to do this. Thus we retrace our steps back to the Wellington site along the even grade, with a view of the highway across the Tye River Valley.

To get to the Wellington site from Seattle, take Interstate 90 east to Interstate 405 and go north 13 miles and take Bothell exit to State Route 522 toward Monroe. At Monroe join Highway 2 going east to Wenatchee via Stevens Pass. Stop at Stevens Pass summit. Retrace west from the summit about ¼ mile for a hairpin turn off highway to access road that winds almost a mile down toward the concrete snowshed just beyond the Wellington site. The old moss-covered concrete snowshed at Tye still stands as a monument to man's attempt to conquer the winter Cascade Mountain snows—and to the Wellington dead.

The trail begins at Wellington and goes west along the old road bed. It first enters the concert showshed and proceeds for almost a mile under cover. It then follows along a high concrete retaining wall of almost the same length. Here the undergrowth gets thicker. Upon approaching Windy Point one is greeted by the 1200 foot long tunnel. From here a trail is planned to go down the steep hillside to the town of Senic on the Stevens Pass Highway; however, trail easements have yet to be obtained to do this. Thus we retrace our steps back to the Wellington site along the even grade, with a view of the highway across the Tye River Valley.

To get to the Wellington site from Seattle, take Interstate 90 east to Interstate 405 and go north 13 miles and take Bothell exit to State Route 522 towards Monroe. At Monroe join Highway 2 going east to Wenatchee via Stevens Pass. Stop at Stevens Pass summit. Retrace west from the summit about one-fourth mile for a hairpin turn off highway to access road that winds almost a mile down towards the concrete snowshed just beyond the Wellington site.

British Columbia

7

British Columbia is the only Canadian province included in our book. The area is dominated by more mountain ranges than Oregon and Washington. Running generally north and south, ranges include the Rocky Mountains forming part of the eastern boundary, the Coast Range in the western section and smaller ranges that include the Selkirks in the south. Its indented Pacific Ocean coastline of 7,000 miles has many inlets and rivers that provide safe harbors for boats and spawning grounds for thousands of salmon.

This territory, like Washington, was first explored by the Spaniards. Captain James Cook first came into contact with the Pacific Northwest when he landed at Nootka on Vancouver Island in 1778. In 1792 Captain George Vancouver explored and mapped much of this coast. The following year Alexander Mackenzie was the first to travel to the Pacific and traveled to Bella Coola, British Columbia, north of Vancouver Island.

This province is famous for its striking contrasts. There is industry as well as extensive untapped natural resources. Massive hydroelectric developments are inland, while extensive fishing takes place off rugged western shores. Arctic weather freezes its northern border, while flowers bloom in the winter at Victoria, the southern tip of Vancouver Island.

British Columbia is big. It runs about 750 miles, north to south, and about 900 miles east and west—almost one and a half times larger than Texas. Thus very little is known or documented regarding hiking trails for the entire province. One project that documented part of the known trails in southwestern British Columbia took six years. One of the areas was Garibaldi Provincial Park, approximately 100 miles wide and 100 miles long.

Although we have visited, camped and hiked different regions here for over twenty years, we have barely scratched the surface. To begin with, the geography of the province, with all of its mountain ranges and steep coastal inlets, does not lend itself to making the region easily accessible. For the outer coast of Vancouver Island, you will require a

BRITISH COLUMBIA

boat or a float plane. A brief check on a map shows how rugged much of the province is.

There are excellent campsite and park areas that have been supported by provincial action and many of those can be used as a base for extensive hiking. We have camped and fished on the Caribou Trail to Prince George and west to Prince Rupert, hiked and beachcombed parts of Vancouver Island, hiked in the Queen Charlottes and gone east to Jasper and Banff. Still, we don't feel that we know this enormous province.

Entrance to Mount Robson Provincial Park near Jasper in eastern British Columbia shows off Mount Robson to full advantage.
British Columbia Government Photograph

A federation of Mountain Clubs of British Columbia assists those who would like to join a hiking club or group. The address is P. O. Box 33768, Vancouver, B. C. V6J 426.

The Manning Provincial Park is one of British Columbia's most magnificent recreational areas. It has about 15 trails from 3 to 30 miles in length or from short walks to 3 days. There is plenty of rugged grandeur variety. The park is 16 miles east of Hope, adjacent to Highway 3.

Mount Robson National Park is west of Jasper. It positively exudes Canadian Rocky Mountain beauty. Many trails of varying length are found here. AT 12,975 feet Mount Robson is the highest peak in the Canadian Rockies.

The Outdoor Club of Victoria has documented selected areas in Vancouver Island from Victoria to Cape Scott via the east coast, including the Pacific Rim National park between Tofino and Ucluelet and Strathcona Provincial Park.

The Queen Charlotte Islands have good hiking and beachcombing. They are a separate island group well off the outer British Columbia coast, about half way to the province's northeast corner of Graham Island.

The underdeveloped land of British Columbia is truly commanding.

Abandoned by the Great Northern Railroad when the Stevens Pass route was lowered, this 4000-feet-long concrete snowshed may now keep hikers dry on proposed trail.

The Wenatchee World photo

The Queen Charlotte Islands, Vancouver Island, the coast of the mainland and the slopes of the Rockies are forested with Douglas fir, cedar, spruce and hemlock. Mountain goat, mule deer, elk and caribou, black bear and grizzlies, ducks, geese, pheasants and grouse provide splendid hunting. Fox and marten, otter, mink and muskrat attract the trapper. Salmon—sockeye, spring, cohoe and chum—come up the rivers to spawn. Several varieties of trout lure anglers to mountain streams and the myriad of inland lakes.

Much backpacking is done in British Columbia along with other activities like fishing and hunting. I think that on the whole, British Columbia appeals not only to the more experienced backpacker, who enjoys a primitive wilderness, but also to the day hiker, who wants to enjoy the rugged scenic beauty.

OLD WEST COAST LIFE-SAVING TRAIL - a challenging trail built for rescuing shipwrecked sailors.

One way: 50 miles; allow seven days backpack.
High point (and elevation gain): 700 feet.
Rain, brush almost impenetrable, making the hike difficult.
Best June through September.
Open all year, but winter travel is hazardous.

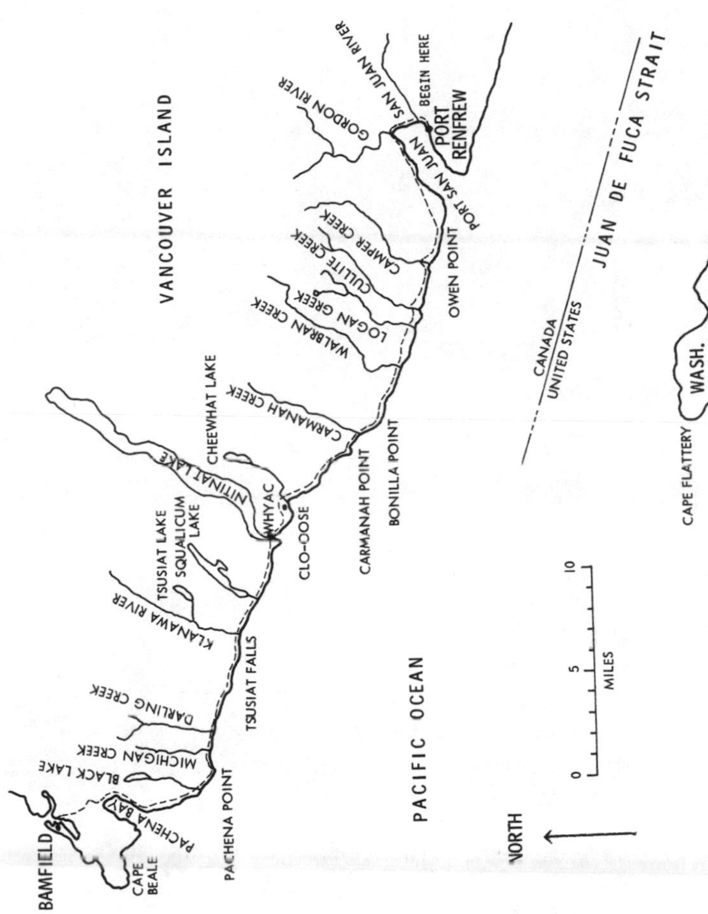

Old West Coast Life Saving Trail

*Remains of the barque **Riata** which foundered near the mouth of the Cheewhat River in 1925. The Cheewhat River footbridge is seen in the background.*

W. H. Gold photo

Six miles west of Nitinat Lake outlet, Tsusiat Falls pours directly onto beach over 80-foot cliff.
W. H. Gold Photo

There is probably no other trail of adventure like this in the world. The Old West Coast Life-Saving Trail, located along the western portion of Canada's Vancouver Island (on the southern coast between Bamfield and Port Renfrew), is a 50-odd-mile trail of unusual historic significance.

Located in the land of the Nitinat Indians, part of the Nootka Nation, the Life-Saving Trail was established in 1890 because of the many shipwrecks that took place on this rugged, almost inaccessible shoreline. Sailing ships making for the Juan de Fuca Straits past Cape Flattery during southwestern Pacific storms would be driven onto these rock-bound shores and ready access was needed to help recover the shipwreck victims, who otherwise would die from injuries or exposure.

Cabins were established along the trail for emergency use by the injured after several sailing vessels were wrecked along the rugged coast and suffered high loss of life. The trail was cut through from both ends and cabins were built about every five miles—each supplied with telephone, medical supplies, blankets, canned food, matches and dry firewood. Additional improvements were made by the government in 1906 following the wreck of the steamer *Valentia,* which resulted in the loss of 126 lives.

To patrol this desolate stretch of coast and to try to keep the telephone line in working order, the Canadian government hired linemen to walk the trail on a regular basis. The line was continually knocked down by windfalls, a casualty of the same Pacific storms that threatened to dash all vessels against this treacherous stretch of rockbound coast. Here the pent-up energy of wind-driven waves, unmolested for 8000 miles, collides head-on with a resisting seacoast; the result seems an attempt to move the unmovable.

Between Port Renfrew and Bamfield an average of one shipwreck has occurred for each mile of its 50-mile stretch. Thus, this region has become known as the "Graveyard of the Pacific," and it quite properly deserves its infamy. In more recent years this same region has continued to claim occasional victims. With the advent of more modern communication and navigation aids, and in the wake of World War II, the need for such a trail lessened. In 1954 the trail was abandoned and maintenance of the trail for life-saving purposes ended. Soon the inevitable windfalls and salal took over.

In 1969 the trail was reopened by Canada's Provincial Parks Branch for recreational hiking purposes. Today the trail is part of Pacific Rim National Park and is maintained by park appropriations. This unusual trail remains a challenge for the hiker seeking the thrill of walking in the footsteps of early shipwreck survivors of the ever-demanding and often violent Pacific.

If the hiker seeks raw Pacific Northwest coastal hiking experience with all its unique problems, he will thoroughly enjoy this route. There are the trials of access across rivers, wide and impassable channels, wet and difficult trails, log jam crossings, slippery rocks and suspension bridges. At one time a ravine had to be crossed in a cart suspended on a long cable. Now there are nine Indian reservations to be transited and a blowdown area (windstorm path where trees are strewn about jackstraw fashion) to be crossed. Indians must be hired to accomplish two river crossings. Campsites are plentiful, and at least five of the original cabins, plus other temporary shelters, are usable.

Of the 50-mile trail, less than ten miles are actual beach hiking, due to impassable coastal rock and cliff areas. Thus most of the hike is inland and out of sight of the ocean. There will be seen, however, the occasional abandoned donkey engine of former logging operations, an abandoned missionary village and the beautiful falls of the Tsusiat River which cascades some 60 feet at the beach edge into the Pacific. Several shipwrecks are still visible east of Pachena Point and at Darling and Michigan Creeks — the last so named for a wrecked ship named Michigan.

Beachcombing along these desolate stretches is excellent. Many a trail hiker has found Japanese glass fishing floats in the driftwood at high tide. The glass balls come in a variety of sizes, from golf to medicine-ball size, and in colors that rival the rainbow. This particular hike provides an excellent opportunity to find such unusual souvenirs — a reminder of the Orient thousands of miles westward.

Careful planning for this hike is very important. Prepare for the incle-

Backpackers hike Old West Coast Life Saving trail on Vancouver Island's outer Pacific Ocean coast. Note unusual wave erosion patterns on shoreline rock of Carmanah Beach.
British Columbia Government photo

ment weather since the annual rainfall is between 100 and 150 inches. Cold winds and heavy, continuous rain may be the norm for any season, practically guaranteeing that the trail will be muddy, that logs will be slippery and that the rivers will be high. Special equipment over and above the usual rain gear required for these conditions includes coastal tide tables, maps, 50 feet of rope, firestarters and flashlights. Bring food for 10 days. Do not plan on eating clams or mussels en route because your hike may coincide with an instance of coastal red tides, which have rendered all bivalves poisonous. Be sure to check with Provincial Fisheries representatives ahead of time, as the beaches infected with red tide may not be posted. There is plenty of fresh water along the trail, so there is no need to carry any.

Wildlife abounds. Along the shore watch for seals, otters, minks and sea lions. Inland, look for marten. Bird life is extensive; eagles abound here. Sighting an osprey, loon or the merganser will be an everyday occurrence. Salmon spawn in the Cheewhat River throughout the year, not solely in the fall season, as Mother Nature usually arranges.

When starting the hike at Port Renfrew, your first day will begin by hiring passage across the Gordon River to shortcut a lengthy trek up one side and back the other. Camper Bay is about seven miles away,

The Blowhole near abandoned village on Old West Coast Life Saving trail of Vancouver Island.
W.H. Gold photo

but other good campsites are available along the way, should you not reach that destination.

On the second day cross the Cullite Creek. The first good place to beachcomb is Logan Creek. From Logan Creek to Carmanah Point are difficult creek crossings. Walbran Creek will require raft crossing, but there is a long, sandy beach trail to Carmanah. This is a very challenging junction.

The third day may take you to Clo-oose, a good stopping place. There are welcome signs of habitation here. This coastal missionary-resort ghost town was alive in the 1940s. At Whyac Indian Reserve hire Nitinat Indians for transportation across the narrows — don't try it yourself.

By the fourth day you should get to the Klanawa River. En route you will see the beautiful Tsusiat Falls cascading into the Pacific. Here the trail again goes inland to the bridge across the river. Good camping and a welcome cabin are available at the Klanawa River mouth.

For the fifth day try for Michigan Creek, where there are several shipwrecks to be seen at low tide. Beachwalking is easy here compared with the earlier portion of the trail.

On the sixth day the trip from Michigan Creek to Pachena Bay is an easy hike—about seven miles. One mile beyond Michigan Creek is the Pachena Light, where there is a register to sign. At the northwest corner of Pachena Bay you will meet the gravel road at the Bible camp.

On the seventh day do the last three miles into Bamfield, consider this trail mastered—and bask in your achievement. There are many other scenic short hikes south to Cape Beale and vicinity if you are so inclined and have the extra time.

If this entire trail sounds too rugged and too adventurous for your liking, the many lakes in the region provide ready access by float plane. In this manner a part of the total trail challenge may be accomplished.

To get there from Vancouver, take a ferry or fly to Victoria on Vancouver Island. There is bus service from Victoria along the south shore to Sooke, Jordan River and Port Renfrew—a total distance of about 66 miles. From Sooke to Port Renfrew the road is restricted for the last 25 miles, meaning it is open to public travel only after logging hours.

To get back, leaving Bamfield you may take the ferry *Lady Rose*, or take the logging road to Port Alberni located at the north end of the 40-mile long salt water canal. Port Alberni, an inland shipping terminus, has friendly people, wide streets and good shopping. Here there is bus service to Nanaimo, where you can catch a ferry that will take you to Horseshoe Bay on the mainland some 10 miles north of downtown Vancouver. Or you can take a public bus from Nanaimo to Victoria if that was your starting point and you didn't have time to see the sights of that delightful British Columbia Province capitol city. But that is another story . . . .

QUEEN CHARLOTTE ISLANDS - where totem poles originated.

One way: 50 miles; allow four to five days.
High point: 500 feet.
Easy but lengthy sea level beach hike.
Open June through September.

Captain John Meares, during his fur trading expedition to the Pacific Northwest in 1778, was the first explorer to record the existence of carved poles, great wooden images that were built by the Haida Indian Nation. This art is believed to have originated on Langara Island at the northwest corner of the Queen Charlotte Islands. From here the practice of carving totems spread to other Indian Nations. The poles later were reported on the mainland as far north as Yakutat, Alaska, inland up the Skeena River at Kispiox, British Columbia and south on the Nootkas at Vancouver Island. Although these carvings initially may have had religious significance, they took on great social and political importance. Today in the Queen Charlotte Islands a few poles can be found at Skidegate Mission, Haida, and in some abandoned villages.

The adze, a tool obtained from fur trading European and American ships, a supply of Western red cedar and slave labor all contributed to the spread of this art. The art of totem poles is felt to be the only art form that Indian men attended to exclusively. Weaving, jewelry making and basketry were done by women.

Building of totem poles subsided in the 1880s, thanks to the abolition of slavery, ravages of smallpox, outlawing of the potlatch, missionary influence and basic changes in the social structure of the Indian family household.

We plan to hike the beach perimeter of the Naikoon Provincial Park. The park is located in the northeast corner of Graham Island, one of the more inaccessible hiking areas of the Pacific Northwest. This hike starts on North Beach, near the village of Haida, goes out to Rose Spit and then winds south to Tlell. This is a sea-level trail. In certain places, the trail is adjacent to the beach, elsewhere it becomes the beach. The adjoining land is rolling lowland, partly covered with dense second-growth timber, while other parts have sparse growth. Much of the area is featureless except for some 25-foot high sand hills.

The Queen Charlottes are located about 60 miles out into the Pacific beginning at Prince Rupert on the British Columbia mainland. Surface vessel and air service is available from Prince Rupert to Masset. There also is surface vessel and air service from Vancouver. From Vancouver, Northland Navigation Co., Ltd. operates two ships to Masset via Prince Rupert. Pacific Western Airlines fly daily except Wednesday, to Sandspit on Moresby Island.

Of the four ways to get to the islands, the most efficient is to fly from Vancouver to Sandspit and continue by land transportation to Masset. From the Sandspit airport you can take a bus or taxi six miles

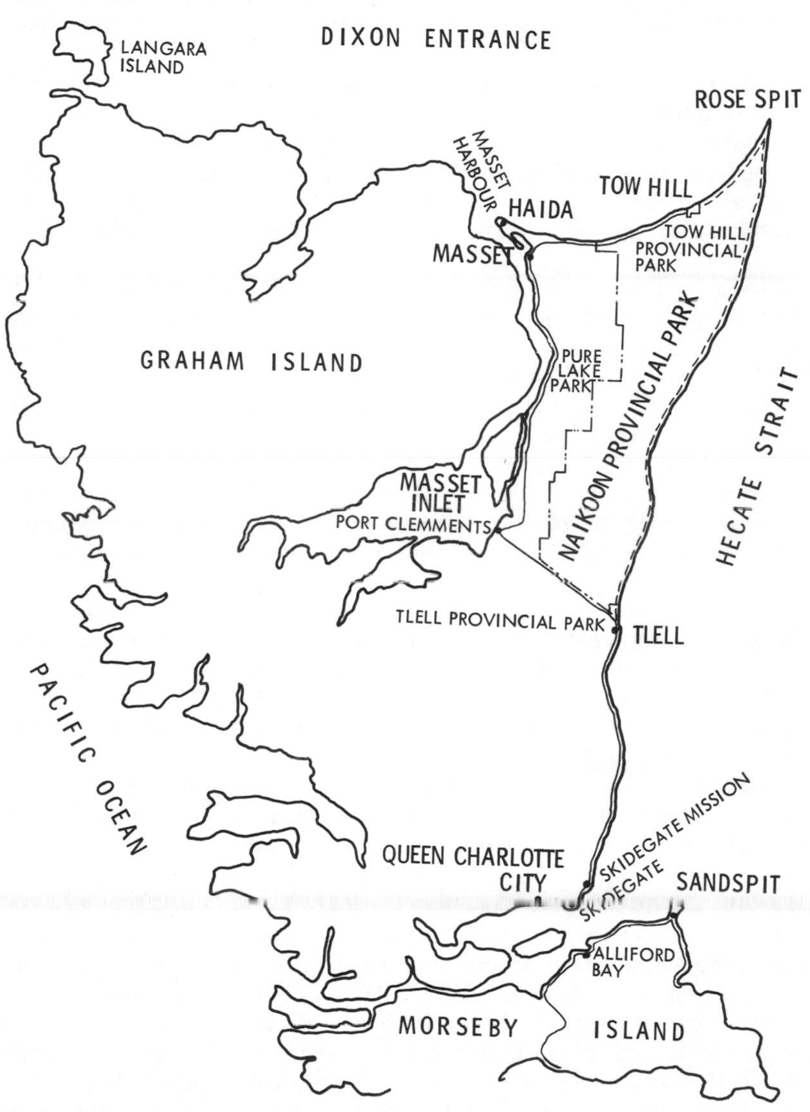

Queen Charlotte Islands

to Alliford Bay, where a two-mile ferry trip across Skidegate Inlet brings you to Skidegate Landing. Nearby to the west is Queen Charlotte City that has approximately 850 inhabitants, a hospital, government offices, stores, charter services and transportation connections. Nearby to the east is Skidegate Mission, an Indian reservation, where approximately 300 Haidas reside.

Daily bus service is available at Queen Charlotte City to Masset, which is about 60 miles north. The road runs along the east shore of Graham Island, which borders Hecate Strait, for about 20 miles to Tlell, the beginning of the Naikoon Provincial Park. Here there is the world famous Tlell River, with its superb fishing. The Tlell Provincial Park is located about two miles north and encompasses the river mouth and spit.

Beyond the Tlell River the road turns inward about 12 miles to Port Clemments, on Masset Inlet, with a community of about 400. There are marine and store services. In another 15 miles north is Pure Lake Park, which has picnic and rest facilities.

The final 15 miles brings you to Masset, a village of about 1700 people. Here are marine and transportation services as well as lodging and stores. A short distance north along Masset Harbour is Haida, the Indian Reservation of about 750. This is the headquarters of the Haida Indian Nation. In the past, Haida was the site of a vast transportation network, and its 8,000 inhabitants, in some 17 villages, were strong politically and economically until the small pox epidemic in the 1880s.

North Beach extends east, about 28 miles, from Haida to Rose Spit. Going east from Masset is a road to Tow Hill Provincial Park, 16 miles away. Tow Hill is a 500-foot-high rock outcropping, a prominent landmark for beach hikers and commercial fishermen and is readily distinguised from the low terrain. It is well worth the hike to the top, where you can photograph the fine view.

Another 10 miles along a drift-filled beach and beachcombers' heaven will bring you to Rose Spit, a low sandy point extending north about two miles that is covered with tiny strawberry plants. This spit catches all sorts of drift on its two sides from Alaskan storms, which occasionally blow at 100 miles per hour.

If the weather is favorable and your provisions are adequate, you then can head south down the east coast for the 40-mile trek to Tlell. Miles of relatively protected sand hills, with some clay cliffs, stretch along a wide flat beach. Here the hiker will beachcomb more glass fishing floats and other strange oriental items. There is an occasional stream to cross, but none is impassable. Wild cattle frequent this northeast region of Graham Island and may startle you. Water may be a problem since some streams originate from low inland brackish sources. The readily visible shipwreck *Pezuta* signals your approach toward the Tlell River as well as the road back to Queen Charlotte City.

At low tide clams can be dug up, assuming there is no red-tide clo-

South of Tlell on the east shore of Graham Island is tail wreckage of World War II bomber high in the driftwood.

Author photo

Residents of Masset paint designs on Japanese glass fishing floats found while hiking North Beach after winter storms.

Author photo

On east shore of Rose Spit beach hiker shows handmade oar used in Indian dugout found after a storm. Large tree was also beached during same storm.

Author photo

sure. (Red tides may poison the clams.) Be sure to check with provincial officials in Masset. You also should check with Forest Service officials regarding camp fires. The hike would be incomplete without fishing some of the streams, so pick up your nonresident license at Masset. Many birds will be seen, and eagles are prevalent. Deer are seen on the beaches.

There are many other places in the Queen Charlotte Islands to visit and hike, however they may require a boat with emergency equipment. In any event, not very many hikers can say, "We climbed Tow Hill, crossed Rose Spit and fished the Tlell."

THE TELEGRAPH TRAIL - an abandoned grand scheme in the wilds of northern British Columbia

One way: 30 miles; allow five days backpack.
High point: 4000 feet.
Elevation drop: 2000 feet.

The Telegraph Trail

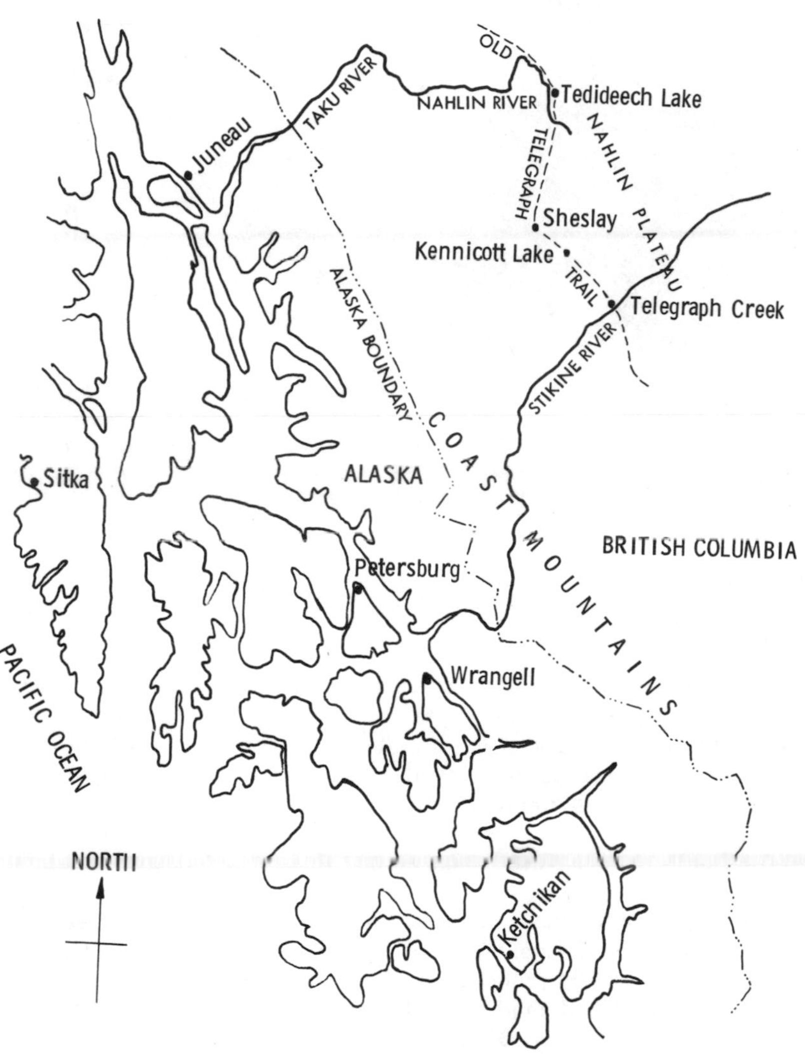

Hiker compares early British manufactured porcelain telegraph insulator with more modern glass type. Porcelain insulators were used during construction of the Collins Telegraph Line in the 1860's in upper British Columbia.

Author photo

Open, dry, low underbrush.
Suggested party: minimum group of four.
Open July-September.

Upon failure of the first Atlantic telegraph cable in 1858, the Collins Overland Telegraph Company was formed to undertake perhaps the most imaginative project of its day. It was to construct a 14,000-mile telegraph line to Europe by an overland line from New York City to San Francisco, then north and westward via a wilderness route through British Columbia and across Alaska's Bering Strait. From here it was to follow Russia's Amur River, then across Russia to Moscow and London.

The originator of this grandiose idea was American Congressman Percy McDonough Collins, who had envisioned the need for an international telegraph link to promote worldwide commerce. The governments of Russia, the United States and Canada all approved the plan, and Western Union Telegraph Company put up the money.

Upwards of $3,000,000 was spent on this project in British Columbia between in 1864 and 1866. The construction party of 250 men had reached Kispiox, B.C., a point 380 miles northwest of Quesnel, British Columbia, on the June, 1866 day when news arrived along the wire they had laid of the successful completion of the second Atlantic cable.

Cabins are still standing that were built every few miles along the Collins Overland Telegraph trail. These cabins housed relay station equipment and provided shelter for line maintenance men. Many like this one are in good shape after 110 years.
Bob Chadwick photo

With that news, work on the overland project ceased. Word didn't get to the crews working the Russian portion until four months later; they completed their link ahd in 1871 that section was extended to Nagasaki, Shanghai and Hong Kong.

Immense stores of wire and poles for continuing the project northward from Kispiox were abandoned in 1867. Exploration of the route had progressed into upper British Columbia about 60 miles east of Juneau, Alaska, to Telegraph Creek, then named for the location where the line would cross the Stikine River.

Although the Collins project was stopped, substantial dividends resulted. The exploration of hundreds of miles of wilderness materially aided the United States in the purchase of Alaska. And western Canada acquired its first telegraph service.

As the Alaskan gold rush brought thousands of people into this part of the world some 30 years later, an urgent need for a telegraph system was met by reviving the Quesnel-Kispiox line and extending it past Atlin, British Columbia, to Dawson City in the Yukon. This telegraph line operated until 1935, when radio replaced it.

Much of the original telegraph line is still visible in upper British Columbia, where hundreds of miles of line were completed. From Quesnel to Kispiox 9246 poles were erected, telegraph lines were strung, and stations were constructed—all in four months' time. The construction party on this portion consisted of 60 white men; 32 Chinese employed as cooks, polemen and wiremen; and 20 Indians employed as boatmen in the transportation of supplies. The organization was highly efficient and military in nature—it had its own magistrate. It was reported that Confederate prisoners of war were employed during early phases of construction.

The telegraph line follows a well-defined trail. Most of the poles carrying insulators are rotted out, but the wire winds on for miles and miles. What makes this trail even more unusual is that many of the log cabin stations still stand. These cabins were later used by the maintenance linemen, perhaps every month, to keep the line open. Some of these cabins have newspapers tacked up for insulation purposes that contain news stories and trivia from the 1920s.

To hike one portion of the "Old Telegraph Trail," as it is designated on British Columbia Topographic maps, start at Tedideech Lake southeast of Nahlin. This is plateau country at about 4000-feet elevation; it is reached by air charter from Juneau, 135 miles west. The destination is Sheslay, a mining town at the turn of the century, 35 miles south.

The trail is good; the telegraph line was constructed nearby. This game trail is in good condition, thanks to the animal traffic. The trail provides easy hiking in the high areas, on ridges and along hills, but once it comes to marshy areas it disappears with no definite direction. This is because the game disperse at such places. One must find the trail at the other side of the marsh. Sometimes this takes a little doing,

Rainbow trout up to 20 inches provided delicious additions to the menu of backpacking group while hiking the Collins Telegraph Line.

Bob Chadwick photo

particularly if the telegraph wire is off to one side. The poles and wire are readily visible only about a quarter of the time.

The locale is generally dry with lodgepole pine and aspen in rolling flat country. Such vegetation and the many lakes make for exceptionally fine fall color scenes to be captured on film. At marshy places the willow grow about five feet high, but on the whole there is generally good visibility ahead without the underbrush that accompanies wetter regions of British Columbia.

Expect to see moose, caribou, marmot and lots of rabbits. Porcupines also frequent this area, judging by the evidence of items having been chewed up along the trail. The trail is used by wolves, but they are timid, stay away from people and are not considered dangerous. Bears are around, but they are not seen very often: they follow the salmon up the rivers later in the year but do not seem to be a problem during the July through September period. Nevertheless, it is always a good rule to avoid areas where fresh bear tracks are found. Just in case, hikers always cache their food by rope up a tree. Another tip: the mosquitoes can be ferocious, so remember the repellent.

Fishing is excellent; cutthroat trout up to 20 inches long are caught in many of the streams almost as fast as you can wet the line. A British Columbia fishing license is required.

Near one cabin several kennels with wooden roofs covered with sod were dug into the ground, indicating the use of dogsled teams during the winter season for transportation. This and other signs provide ample evidence of cold winters and considerable snow.

For a typical day along the trail, enjoy an after-breakfast hike of seven miles following the telegraph line, visiting cabins and exploring adjacent areas. Stop by a good stream for lunch. Afterwards have a nap, enjoy the scenery, explore (during a side trip) and catch fish for dinner. After dinner, as darkness closes in, listen to the evening sounds of the wilderness.

This is one fine place to get the feeling of being out by yourself, 75 miles from the nearest inhabited cabin or help. It is an interesting experience to be dropped into an area that has not been visited by anyone else for the past year. You are on your own, so take care here with knives, axes or hatchets, and watch your footing.

Sheslay, the destination, was abandoned in about 1920. A few broken-down buildings remain to suggest signs of former habitation. Artifacts of that era lay as they were left more than 50 years ago—old crosscut saws, tools long since rusted, hand-made sleds. There is also a more modern touch: an airstrip that was cut out of the growth along the river edge. But it too has been deserted.

Some of the telegraph insulators that are seen all along the line are of white porcelain and are believed to have been manufactured in England. Others were made of blue glass, bearing dates in the 1890s. Both are considered antiques and are collector's items. The wire used for the telegraph lines is steel about three-sixteenths-inch in diameter and quite hard to bend by hand; consequently, not much of this leaves the area.

On the Nahlin River are the remains of a suspension bridge that dates back to the turn of the century. A "corduroy" road leading to this bridge over a long marshy area was undoubtedly used by mule-drawn carts to carry the heavy rolls of telegraph wire. At another location is a long-abandoned ranch with its farm equipment—the nearest road end is 100 miles away.

This hike requires planning. The logistics of the expedition depend on proper preparation. Plan on carrying everything on your back. The hike as described here is generally in a downhill direction. Special equipment to be carried by *each* member includes a detailed map of the entire area plus a pocket compass. Agreement as to the specific location each time camp is set up is essential. The importance of the party's staying together cannot be overstated.

To get there, the easiest way is to fly Alaska Airlines from Seattle to Juneau on the morning flight, which takes about two hours. Lunch in Juneau. Arrange for the gear to be taken to the charter service for loading into the silver Beaver airplane on floats. It will carry five passengers with their gear, a typical bush operation. The trip from Juneau

Backpacking group fords river while following telegraph line trail. Note that hiking boots are carried or tied to the packs.

Bob Chadwick photo

is a spectacular flight over glaciers and lakes and will take about an hour. You land on Tedideech Lake by 3 p.m., in plenty of time to set up camp.

The return air trip is on a similar schedule. By prearrangement you are picked up at Kennicott Lake in the afternoon with your gear and some freshly caught trout, you land at Juneau, catch the return jet dinner flight and arrive in Seattle before dark, trout and all.

Do you worry about being picked up out in the bush by your pilot? No, it is the unwritten law of the charter services in this type of country always to make the appointment, unless impossible weather sets it—in which case the appointment is for the same time next day. The worst that can happen is that you get another day for fishing.

For those with more time who would like to go by ship, the Alaska State Ferries from Seattle reach Juneau in about three days—an enjoyable voyage along the inside passage.

All in all, this is a fascinating hike. The fall scenery in flat-lake, rolling country when the foliage is turning makes for memories. A group can fly in one year, hike 30 miles and return another time to continue where they left off earlier. Longer hikes can be planned for this country, depending on individual speed and pleasure. In any event, where else can one experience the excitement of hiking a quiet trail with continual evidence alongside of an abandoned grandiose plan for international communication?

Southeastern Alaska

8

While hiking in southeastern Alaska you will experience an environment similar to the outer coast of British Columbia, namely difficult access, sometimes violent north Pacific Aleutian weather, exposed rugged coastlines and protected lee beaches.

The hiker is dependent on coastwise ferries and floatplanes to get there. Your bush pilot will drop you off at some point and return for you at an agreed upon place and time. You should go with someone who is familiar with the region. As in British Columbia, most backpacking here is added to other activities, like fishing and hunting.

Only a few can afford to take their own floatplane out to a remote trailhead or beach. If you do fly your own plane, land at an inland lake and beach in a protected salt water cove so that no sudden adverse weather catches you unprepared. Then hike to some nearby area for fishing or a secluded beach to beachcomb. It is always best for one person to stay with the airplane while the other person hikes.

Southeastern Alaska, known as the "panhandle," is mainly a series of islands and channels that project down the western side of British Columbia. Near the coastal towns, most of the terrain begins an ascent up the side of the Coast Range. In this region, the towns of Skagway, Sitka, Juneau, Wrangell and Ketchikan are to be found. In many places glaciers come down to the water's edge and break off into icebergs. Among the most noted glaciers are the Malaspina, at the base of Mount St. Elias, and the Mendenhall glacier, which is north of Juneau. It is a lot easier flying over southeastern Alaska than hiking it.

Regarding its history, Alaska was explored by two Russians, Bering and Chirikof, who sighted the panhandle in 1741. Bering named 18.008-foot Mount St. Elias, located on the international boundary line in southeastern Alaska. Chirikof landed near the present site of Sitka, and Baranof deemed it the territory's capital. In 1867, 125 years later, the United States bought Alaska from Russia. In 1959 Alaska became the 49th state.

Alaska is a land of timber. Forests—chiefly consisting of spruce, hemlock and cedar, with some birch and poplar—cover the coastal re-

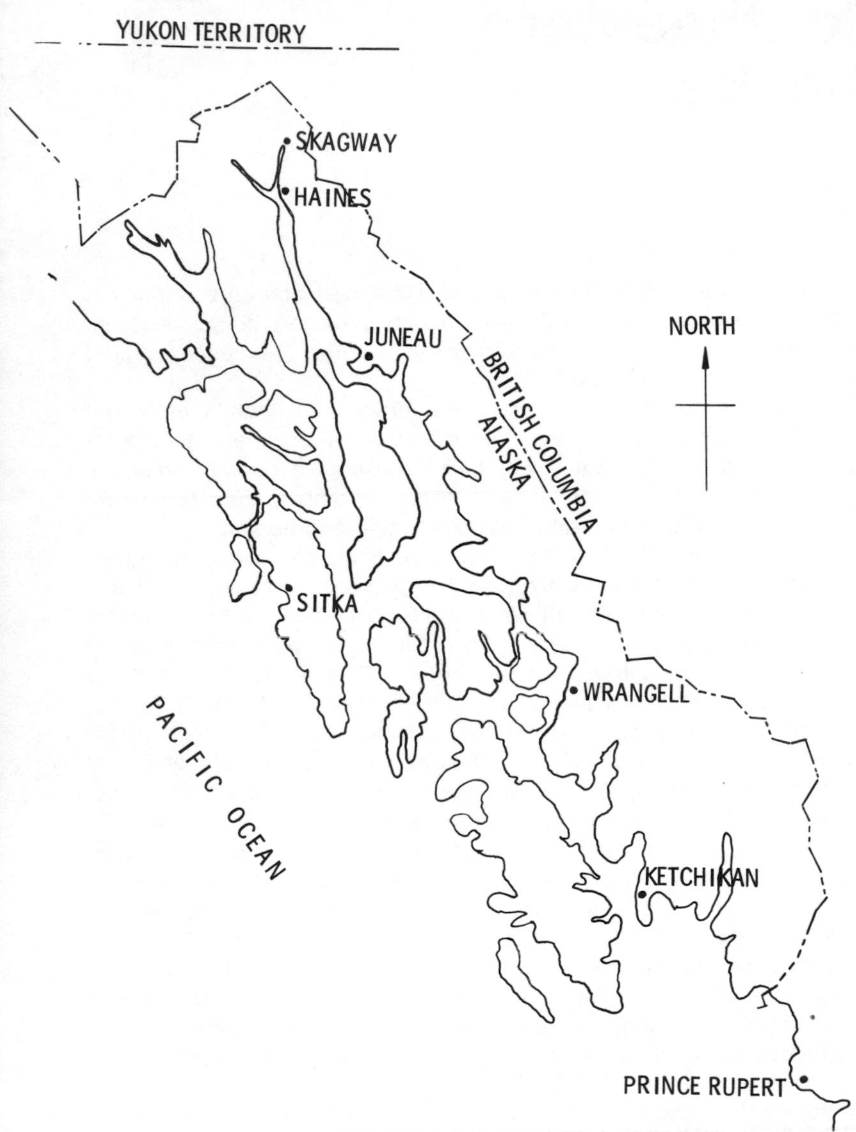

SOUTHEASTERN ALASKA

Much of Alaska's shore consists of rocky areas like this one. The Alaskan beach hiker can enjoy such areas that defy storm, tide, and time. This vista is near Cape Addington in Southeastern Alaska.
Dick Hamlin photo

Beach hiker used backpack to carry Japanese glass fishing floats back to airplane. This is example of good beachcombing at isolated beach in Alaska.

Dick Hamlin photo

gion. Beaver, fox, land otter, marten, mink, ermine, muskrat, seal, wolf and bear are some of the fur-bearing animals found here. The lakes, rivers and coastal waters are abound with fish.

In spring and fall, rainfall is heavy as the ocean winds rise over the coastal mountains. During the spring and summer, wildflowers profusely grow in the valleys.

Three federal agencies—the National Park Service, the U.S. Forest Service and the U.S. Fish and Wildlife Service—administer extensive areas. In the southeastern panhandle, Glacier Bay National Monument and Sitka National Monument can be seen.

The U.S. Forest Service administers Tongass National Forest, which encompasses most of southeastern Alaska. The U.S. Fish and Wildlife Service maintains the Kodiak Bear Refuge and a number of lesser known bird, sea-life and wildlife preserves in the southeast. Numerous campgrounds are maintained by the State of Alaska, Division of Lands, the U.S. Bureau of Land Management, the U.S. Forest Service, the U.S. Fish & Wildlife Service and the U.S. National Parks Service. Additional information can be obtained by writing to the U.S. National Park Service in Juneau, Alaska 99801.

CHILKOOT TRAIL - the historic gold rush trail.

One way: 32 miles; allow four to five days one way.
High Point: 3740 feet.
Elevation gain: 2140 feet.
Rugged trail at upper elevations.
Open July through September.

From 1897 to 1898 some 30,000 prospectors, in their quest for gold against great odds, climbed the Chilkoot Pass to the Klondike gold fields. The stampede began when gold-laden prospectors arrived in Seattle on July 17, 1897, on the *Portland.* The Gold Rush lured many who were blinded by Klondike fever. The world was in the midst of a financial depression, and the gold's glitter beckoned persons of many nationalities—Scotch, Irish, French, German, Canadian and American.

The Chilkoot Pass was the shortest route for these prospectors. The first 32 miles over the pass to Lake Bennett made the rest of the 600 mile trip seem easy. The Chilkoot Pass was a formidable initiation for those who made it all the way to Dawson City. Because the trail went into Canada at the pass, the Royal Canadian Mounted Police required that each person entering Canada have a year's supply of food. Therefore each prospector had to shuttle about one ton of food and gear from Dyea or Skagway up over the pass to Lake Lindeman or Lake Bennett, the navigable headwaters of the northbound Yukon River system. The Mounties also collected customs from the prospectors at each shuttle. Because of the great influx of people and attendant lawlessness, United States troops were sent in to settle disputes in the area between Skagway and the Chilkoot Pass.

Chilkoot Pass

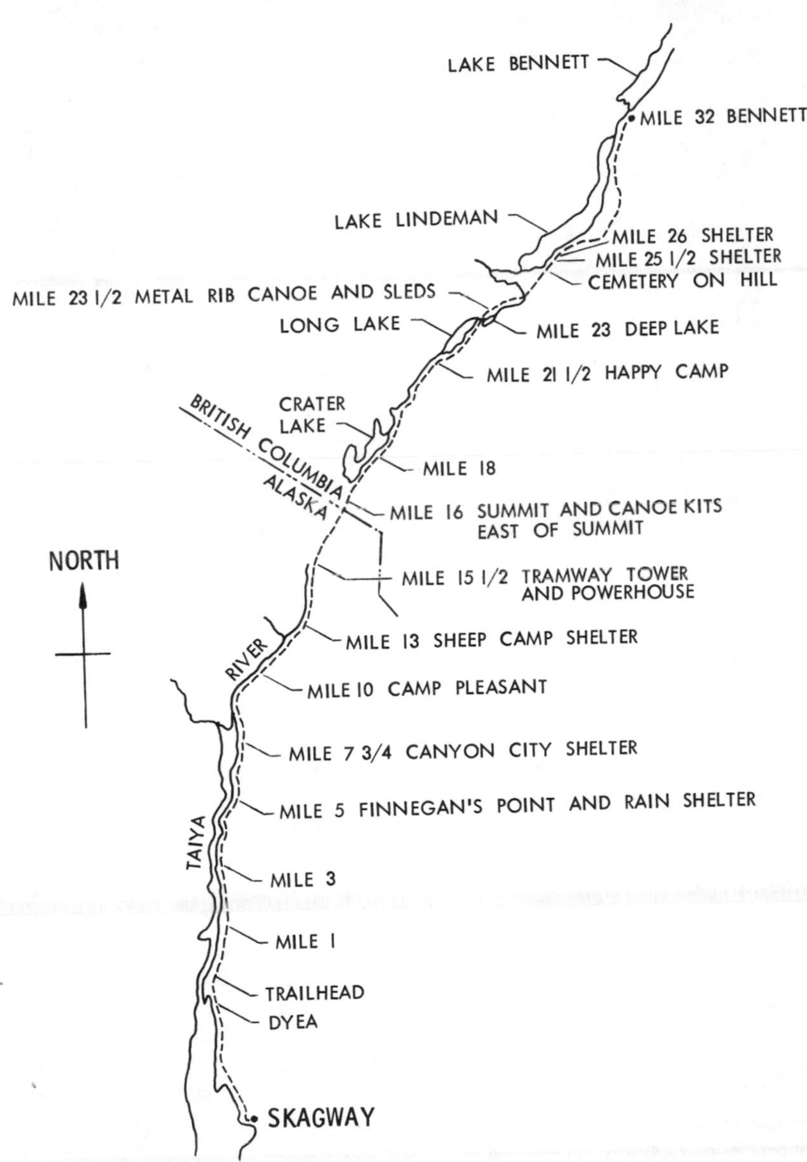

Commemorative plaque seen to the right of the trail on the Alaska side near Chilkoot Pass summit.
Nancy Oyler photo

Horses were used to carry the gear the first 15 miles, from Skagway to Dyea, to where the steep ascent began. For the final assault on the Chilkoot Pass a long line of prospectors climbed steps cut in the snow for the steep 40-degree upward climb. Once in line a prospector dare not rest since the others would not let him back in—so eager were these men to arrive at the gold fields. Once at Lake Bennett, where boats were built, the rest of the trip could be made by water.

After the gold rush the Chilkoot Trail fell into disuse and stayed alive only in the memories of those who lived to cross it. The White Pass and Yukon Route Railway had been completed between Skagway and Whitehorse in 1900 over a route that closely paralled the Chilkoot Trail. The town of Dyea was abandoned, but Skagway kept going as a water and rail transportation terminus for inland mining operations. Later in the 1920s it became a popular stop for tourist vessels. Sightseeing day trips were made available on this railway to Lake Bennett, Whitehorse and back. This railroad now operates daily in the summer, except on Sundays and holidays, and is the major transportation outlet for Yukon freight.

In the 1930s a group of citizens from Skagway petitioned the National Park Service for a national park or monument including Skag-

Uncompleted Presbyterian church on hill overlooking Lake Bennett.

Duane Oyler photo

Hundreds of knocked down wood and canvas canoe kits abandoned 75 yards east of summit of Chilkoot Pass on rock ledge.

Duane Oyler photo

way, Dyea and the Chilkoot Pass. In 1959, when Alaska was admitted as a state, the idea was revived. Soon the Canadian Government indicated a desire to cooperate on that portion of the trail north of the pass. Shelters have been constructed, footbridges added and trail markers established. Now U.S. Park Service rangers are assigned to the trail between Dyea and Chilkoot Pass.

Most backpackers make the trip as the gold rush prospectors did—from Skagway up over the Chilkoot Pass to Bennett—and then return by rail. It would be considerably easier to hike it in the reverse direction from Bennett to Skagway. You would start at 2100 feet, climb to 3740 feet and then coast down to sea level. When you arrive at Skagway by Alaska ferry, the sights can be seen quickly. A grocery store has supplies if needed. An eight-mile taxi ride takes you to Dyea, where the trailhead is located.

Once under way on the trail, you must take a steep climb for part of the first mile. The trail then levels off—high above the Taiya River. Soon it drops to the river's level. For the first three miles the hike is relatively easy, partly on a muddy logging road and goes to an abandoned sawmill with some storage sheds. At Finnegan's Point, western glaciers provide a beautiful view.

View looking north into British Columbia and Yukon Territory from top of Chilkoot Pass.

Duane Oyler photo

Trail sign at top of Chilkoot Pass. Worn out rubber boot lies discarded from Gold Rush days.
Nancy Oyler photo

The Canyon City shelter has been established by Alaska's Department of Natural Resources. This shelter has eight bunks and is often the first stop on the trail. Beyond this shelter and off the trail are the ruins of the original Canyon City townsite.

Beyond Canyon City is another steep climb and then it bears down again to the river and Camp Pleasant. Three more easy miles brings you to Sheep Camp shelter, which is similar to the previous one. This shelter has artifacts and relics all over. From here the trail heads up toward the summit. In about two miles the trail veers out from the trees and snow banks are encountered.

On the west side of the pass, at the 15½ mile, is a tramway tower and collapsed building and snowfield. Here you climb on rock, and it is quite steep. After a series of climbs and descents, the trail drops into a bowl-like area immediately below the final ascent, called the Scales. Here are lots of relics, cast offs from the Gold Rush. After a rock climb the summit is reached through a narrow gap. The commemorative plaque is located a short distance from the summit on the right. Abandoned canoe kits are seen on a ledge to the right. Here the view is rarely clear. Poor visibility and whiteout are common.

In one and one-half miles is Crater Lake. Between Crater Lake and Long Lake the trail goes through a quarter-mile long canyon alongside a stream with loose rocks. Be careful here. Happy Camp is just be-

Sheep Camp shelter cabin on Chilkoot trail. Cabin has Gold Rush relics hanging outside and others for inside use.

Duane Oyler photo

Nancy Oyler photo

yond. Deep Lake is another one and one-half miles. A footbridge takes the trail to the river's west side. At the 23rd mile is a campsite. Another half mile brings you to the metal frame of a boat and several pieces of sleighs.

When you approach Lake Lindeman, look for the Ranger Station and two cabins at the lake's south end. Here is a considerable number of relics. It is another seven miles to Bennett. On the way a cemetery and an uncompleted church can be seen.

After a prospector's lunch is served in the station restaurant, consisting of stew, bread and apple pie—all of which is included in the price of a train ticket—the train leaves Bennett and arrives at Skagway. Reservations are necessary because of cruise-trip bookings. Although you might see few hikers on the trail, 30 or more will converge on the station to eat lunch and catch the train.

The weather in July may be overcast on the Skagway side, closed in at the pass and clear on the Canadian side. Be prepared for wet weather during the entire trip. August weather might be clear or miserable.

The Chilkoot trail is generally well marked. There are interpretative markers, sealed frames about two by three feet on stands, that contain photographic enlargements taken during the gold rush with English and French captions. On the trail you can relate to the hardships that befell the prospectors.

To reach the Chilkoot Trail from Seattle, most hikers travel on one of the Alaska ferries. The MV *Columbia* departures at 9 p.m., Friday; stops at Ketchikan, Wrangell and Petersburg on Sunday; Sitka on Monday and Juneau, Haines and Skagway on Tuesday. The Canadian National's *Prince George* has a similar schedule out of Vancouver.

Chilkoot Pass hiker enters Skagway down main street where railroad once ran.

Duane Oyler photo

Dave Smith photo

Postscripts

So you have now walked with Lewis and Clark, followed covered wagon trails, beachcombed the Pacific, admired alpine meadows, viewed majestic snowcapped mountains, watched the migration of the grey whale and followed the spawning salmon. This is just an introduction to many more hiking experiences to be had in the Pacific Northwest. There are hundreds of glaciers to photograph, many profiles of prominent mountains to enjoy, upland lakes to fish and unusual geologic formations to wonder at.

Here are our choices of some of the exciting hiking trails available throughout the entire Pacific Northwest—trails we selected because of their historical or geographical significance, not for their popularity. Thus our choices will differ from those found in other regional hiking literature.

The trails were selected to appeal to newcomers to the region, to young family groups already here, the senior citizen groups, even the newcomer to hiking. Thus the predominence of day trips. Yet there are a few challenges, like the Old West Coast Life Saving Trail and the Chilkoot Pass Trail, that should whet the appetite of the experienced backpacker.

In this guide, we have suggested a few places to hike. The book is not intended to be a definitive work on the basics of how to backpack or what gear to buy. The bibliography contains excellent source material for further study covering a broad spectrum of hiking interest.

The Pacific Northwest is a vast and beautiful country. It does not have to be experienced to be appreciated. Perhaps the hiker of the northeast, mid-Atlantic states, Southern Mountains and the midwest will be persuaded through these readings to join us at a Pacific Ocean beach or in a Cascade Alpine meadow.

Our immediate family has spent many pleasant hours hiking the Pacific Northwest and has developed a love for the ammenities provided by this region. The woodsy odors, the beauty of the Indian paintbrush bloom, the grandeur of a snowcapped peak—all bring a singular inner peace not easily described.

We, too, have shared the excitement when trying out a new trail. First, the anticipation during the "armchair cruising" over maps and references; secondly, the actual hike planning; and finally, the doing. Our photographs that we share spur our plans for future outings.

I like to bring home an occasional souvenir from my trips. To me, an acorn from the trail, an agate from the beach and a maple leaf from the foothills are reminders of enjoyable outings. Once I brought back a piece of sagebrush during a hike near Ellensburg, Washington. When I would break off a small twig, the sage odor permeated the air and clung to my finger tips.

The Pacific Northwest is truly a hiker's paradise. We hope you enjoyed taking a walk with us over this large region with its beaches, foothills, and alpine meadows. By following simple safety cautions and by being certain that we leave no traces of our presence—it can remain a truly heavenly place for those who may follow.

Bibliography

Angier, Bradford. *How to Live in the Woods for Pennies a Day.* Harrisburg: Stackpole Books, 1971.

Adney, Edwin Tappan. *The Klondike Stampede of 1897 - 1898.* Fairfield: Ye Galleon Press, 1968.

Balcom, Mary. *Ghost Towns of Alaska.* Chicago: Adams, 1965.

Becky, Fred W. *Challenge of the North Cascades.* Seattle: Mountaineers, 1969.

Becky, Fred W. and Bjornstad, Eric. *Guide to Leavenworth Rock Climbing Areas.* Seattle: Mountaineers, 1965.

Berton, Pierre. *Klondike.* Toronto: McClelland and Stewart Limited, 1972.

Bjornstad, Eric and Becky, Fred W. *Guide to Leavenworth Rock Climbing Areas.* Seattle: Mountaineers, 1965.

Bullard, Oral and Lowe, Don. *Short Trips and Trails, The Columbia Gorge.* Beaverton: Touchstone Press, 1974.

Carey, Neil. *A Guide to the Queen Charlotte Islands.* Seattle: Alaska Northwest, 1975.

Cook, Jimmie Jean. *A Particular Friend, Penn's Cove.* Coupeville: Island County Historical Society, 1973.

Cyca, Robert and Harcombe, Andrew. *Exploring Manning Park.* Vancouver: Gundy's and Bernie's Guide Books, 1973.

Dalzell, Kathleen. *The Queen Charlotte Islands 1774 - 1966.* Terrace: C.M. Adam, 1968, republished Cove Press, 1973.

Dalzell, Kathleen. *The Queen Charlotte Islands Book 2 of Places and Names.* Prince Rupert: Cove Press, 1973.

Darvill, Fred T., M.D. and Marshall, Louise B. *Winter Walks.* Lynnwood: Signpost Publications, 1970.

Feris, Charles. *Hiking the Oregon Skyline.* Beaverton: Touchstone Press, 1973.

Fish, Byron. *60 Unbeaten Paths.* Seattle: Superior, 1972.

Fleming, June. *The Well-Fed Backpacker.* Portland: Victoria House, 1976.

Fletcher, Colin. *The Complete Walker.* New York: Knopf, 1969.

Garvey, Edward B. *Hiking Trails in the Mid-Atlantic States.* Matteson: Greatlakes Living Press, 1976.

Gray, William. *The Pacific Crest Trail.* National Geographic Society, 1975.

Hancock, David and Sterling, David. *Pacific Wilderness.* Saanichton: Hancock House Publishers, 1974.

Harcombe, Andrew and Cyca, Robert. *Exploring Manning Park.* Vancouver: Gundy's and Bernie's Guide Books, 1973.

Hazard, Joseph T. *Pacific Coast Trails from Alaska to Cape Horn.* Seattle: Superior, 1946.

Henley, Thomas A. and Sweet, Neesa. *Hiking Trails in the Northeast.* Matteson: Greatlakes Living Press, 1976.

Horn, Elizabeth. *The Cascades.* Beaverton: Touchstone Press, 1972.

Jansen, Charles. *Lightweight Backpacking.* New York: Bantam, 1974.

Keithahn, Edward L. *Monuments in Cedar.* Ketchikan: Roy Anderson, 1945, republished Seattle: Suverior, 1963.

Kemp, J. Larry. *Epitaph for the Giants.* Portland: Touchstone Press, 1967.

Kirk, Ruth. *Exploring Crater Lake Country.* Seattle: University of Washington Press, 1975.

Kirk, Ruth. *Exploring Mount Rainier.* Seattle: University of Washington Press, 1968.

Kirk, Ruth. *Exploring the Olympic Peninsula.* Seattle: University of Washington Press, 1964.

Kirk, Ruth. *The Olympic Rain Forest.* Seattle: University of Washington Press, 1966.

Krenmayr, Janice. *Footloose around Puget Sound.* Seattle: Mountaineers, 1969.

Leissler, Frederick. *Roads and Trails of Olympic Natuonal Park.* Seattle: University of Washington Press, 1957.

Leslie, Robert. *High Trails West.* New York: Crown Publishers, 1967.

Lowe, Don and Roberta. *100 Northern California Hiking Trails.*Beaverton: Touchstone Press, 1970.

Lowe, Don and Roberta. *70 Hiking Trails, Northern Oregon Cascades.* Beaverton: Touchstone Press, 1974.

Lowe, Don and Bullard, Oral. *Short Trips and Trails, The Columbia Gorge.* Beaverton: Touchstone Press, 1974.

Lyttle, Richard. *The Complete Beginners Guide to Backpacking.* New York: Doubleday, 1975.

Macaree, David. *103 Hikes in Southwestern British Columbia.* Vancouver: British Columbia Mountaineering Club, 1973, and Seattle: Mountaineers.

Macaree, David and Mary. *109 Walks on B.C.'s Lower Mainland.* Seattle: Mountaineers, 1976.

Manning, Harvey. *Backpacking One Step at a Time.* Seattle: REI Press, 1972.

Manning, Harvey. *Mountaineering, the Freedom of the Hills*. Seattle: Mountaineers, 1969. (Planned by Climbing Committee of the Mountaineers.)

Manning, Harvey and Spring, Ira. *101 Hikes in the North Cascades*. Seattle: Mountaineers, 1970.

Manning, Harvey. *The Wild Cascades Forgotten Parkland*. San Francisco: Sierra Club, 1965.

Marshall, Louise. *A Guide to the Pacific Crest National Scenic Trail*. Lynnwood: Signpost Publications, 1972.

Marshall, Louise. *High Trails*. Seattle: University of Washington Press, 1962.

Marshall, Louise. *100 Hikes in Western Washington*. Seattle: Mountaineers, 1966.

Marshall, Louise. *Winter Walks Near Seattle and Everett*. Seattle: Signpost Publications, 1971.

Marshall, Louise and Darvill, Fred T., M.D. *Winter Walks*. Lynnwood: Signpost Publications, 1970.

Mendenhall, Ruth Dyar. *Backpack Cookery*. Glendale: La Siesta, 1974.

Mendenhall, Ruth Dyar. *Backpack Techniques*. Glendale: La Siesta, 1967.

Mitchell, Dick. *Mountaineering First Aid*. Seattle: Mountaineers, 1972.

Morgan, Murray. *One Man's Gold Rush*. Seattle: Universify of Washington Press, 1967.

Nicholson, George. *Vancouver Island's West Coast*. Victoria: Morriss Printing Company Ltd., 1963.

Outdoor Club of Victoria. *Hiking Trails III, Central and Northern Vancouver Island, Including Hiking Routes of Strathcona Park*. Victoria: Outdoor Club of Victoria, 1975.

Pattison, Ken. *Milestones on Vancouver Island*. Victoria: Milestone, 1973.

Prater, Gene. *Snowshoeing*. Seattle: Mountaineers, 1974.

Ratliff, Donald E. *Map, Compass and Campfire*. Portland: Binfords & Mort, 1964.

Rossit, Edward. *Northwest Mountaineering*. Caldwell: Caxton Printers 1965.

Satterfield, Archie. *Chilkoot Pass: Then and Now*. Anchorage: Alaska Northwest Publishing Company, 1973.

Schwartz, Susan. *Cascade Companion*. Seattle: Pacific Search, 1976.

Sierra Club of British Columbia. *The West Coast Trail & Nitinat Lakes*. Vancouver: J.J. Douglas Ltd., 1972.

Silverman, Goldie. *Backpacking with Babies and Small Children*. Lynnwood: Signpost Publication, 1975.

Spring, Ira and Manning, Harvey. *50 Hikes in Mount Rainier National Park*. Seattle: Mountaineers, 1975.

Spring, Ira and Manning, Harvey. *101 Hikes in the North Cascades.* Seattle: Mountaineers, 1973.

Spring, Ira and Manning, Harvey. *102 Hikes in the Alpine Lakes, South Cascades and Olympics.* Seattle: Mountaineers, 1971.

Sterling, David and Hancock, David. *Pacific Wilderness.* Saanichton: Hancock House Publishers, 1974.

Sterling, E.M., *Trips and Trails, 1.* Seattle: Mountaineers, 1967.

Sterling, E.M., *Trips and Trails, 2.* Seattle: Mountaineers, 1968.

Stevens, Hazard. *The First Ascent of Takhoma.* The Atlantic Monthly: November, 1876.

Sullivan, Jerry and Daniel, Glenda. *Hiking Trails in the Midwest.* Chicago: Greatlakes Living Press, 1974.

Sullivan, Jerry and Daniel, Glenda. *Hiking Trails in the Southern Mountains.* Matteson: Greatlakes Living Press, 1975.

Sunset. *Sunset Camping Handbook.* Menlo Park: Lane, 1970.

Sutton, Ann and Myron. *The Pacific Coast Trail.* New York: Lippincott, 1975.

Sweet, Neesa and Henley, Thomas A. *Hiking Trails in the Northeast.* Matteson: Greatlakes Living Press, 1976.

Tabor, Rowland W. and Crowder, Dwight. *Routes and Rocks in the Mt. Challenger Quadrangle by Ed Hanson.* Seattle: Mountaineers, 1968.

Wasco County Historical Society and Clackamas County Historical Society. *Barlow Road.* Portland: Wasco County Historical Society and Clackamas County Historical Society, 1976.

Webber, Bert.*Retaliation: Japanese Attacks and Allied Countermeasures on the Pacific Coast in World War 11.* Corvallis: Oregon State University Press, 1975.

Winnett, Thomas, *Backpacking for Fun.* Berkeley: Wilderness Press, 1972.

Wood, Amos L. *Beachcombing for Japanese Glass Floats.* Portland: Binfords & Mort, 1971.

Wood, Amos L. *Beachcombing the Pacific.* Chicago: Henry Regnery, 1975.

Wood, Robert. *Wilderness Trails of Olympic National Park.* Seattle: Mountaineers, 1968.